NAVIGATING *the* WATERS

REBECCA NOLTING

NAVIGATING
the
WATERS

Revealing Faithfulness in Our Voyage With God

ASK PUBLISHING

Pueblo, Colorado

TABLE OF CONTENTS

ACKNOWLEDGMENTS

First, I want to praise God for being faithful every moment of my life. He has been my true north, guiding me in every step of my journey.

Second, I am so grateful for my husband, Jeffrey, who has been my faithful partner in life since we met in 2004. His steadfast love keeps my ship upright in both sunny and stormy days.

Third, I want to thank Pastor Scott Schurle and the team at TLC Book Design for your guidance and support throughout my writing journey. They challenge me to go deeper in my storytelling, seeking God's direction to be more open and candid.

Finally, I want to thank everyone who has encouraged me, lifted me up, prayed for me, and walked with me on my faith journey. You have been beacons of light to guide me in my darkest moments.

LETTER FROM THE AUTHOR

Hello Friend,

Ahoy! A couple of years ago, I was in a Bible study about the fruit of the Spirit. "The fruit of the Spirit is love, joy, peace, forbearance, kindness, goodness, faithfulness, gentleness and self-control. Against such things there is no law" (Galatians 5:22–23). At the end of the study, we were all asked to share which fruit of the Spirit we wanted the group to pray for us. My word was faithfulness. I had been on this writing journey for a few years with a lot of twists and turns. For me, the word faithfulness means "to keep going." Thankfully, one lesson I have seen repeatedly in the Bible and in my life is that God is always faithful, even if we aren't.

Several years ago, God gave me an image of a ship. It took patience and God's timing for me to see the connections between those images and faithfulness. I have found

God uses many ways to get a specific message to me. One way is through watching reality shows, for which my husband teases me about. For me, it's a way to watch something that doesn't require a lot of brain power and to see other people's drama (and escape from my own). One show is a series called *Below Deck*, which is about staff on a super yacht dealing with demanding guests and coworker drama. I kept hearing all the terms for the parts of the boat and for sailing. What struck me is God used a silly reality show to help confirm a writing idea I had.

However, our faith journey isn't all smooth sailing on an expensive boat. Our faithfulness is revealed while we navigate through familiar words ending in -ship, as we cling to our life preserver of Christ. As in my previous books, I have included reflection questions at the end of each chapter to help deepen your faith. I have also included songs to listen to as they are another way we hear from God. Each chapter ends with an act of faithfulness, which is meant to push you to take another step of faith and trust God.

Let's get on board!

Song: "My God Can"

by Katy Nichole & Naomi Raine

PREPARING
for the
JOURNEY

1

GET ON BOARD

"For no word from God will ever fail."

(Luke 1:37)

"SITTING ON THE BEACH staring out at the ocean" is my answer when someone asks me to imagine my favorite peaceful place—waves crashing on the shore, water stretching as far as the eye can see, the warmth of the sun as you run your fingers through the sand, the salty air, a lighthouse, and people splashing in the refreshing water. As you look out to the horizon, you may see a kayak, a sailboat, a fishing vessel, or a container ship. These watercraft need not only a way to propel forward, but a way to navigate to their destination, much like our faith journey. We may not understand where our path is leading us, but God is guiding every step, if we are willing to follow.

What if a man on the shoreline asked you to drop everything and come follow him, like when Jesus called his disciples? What kind of faith would that take? It starts with our willingness to "get on board" and accept Jesus as our Savior. One's experience of being saved may differ from another. I have been asked about the moment when I was saved. I don't have a specific moment that stands out, but I always felt like I knew that Jesus was my Savior. There have been many moments in my life when I felt God's presence drawing me even closer to him. It is a choice we make to seek Jesus every day. He doesn't expect perfection as we all fall short. But God wants us to do our best to remain faithful and seek his guidance in all decisions.

Writing this book was a get-on-board moment, when I had to say "yes" again to God's call. Once again, I was faced with connecting biblical stories with my own faith journey, while showing God's faithfulness in it all. Exploring these biblical stories helps us see that even if the biblical characters might not have done everything perfectly, God still used them to show his love for his people.

It feels fitting to start with the story of Mary and Joseph. While all of us had to choose to get on board with God's plan, Mary and Joseph were given a unique task: to take care of the Son of God. Let's put ourselves in their shoes for a moment. As Mary, you are engaged to be married and an angel comes to you saying you have been called to give birth and raise a man who would be our Savior. As Joseph, you are asked to accept your pregnant fiancée and be a father to this special child. I don't know about you, but I would need a big sign from God, like an angel, to get on board with that challenge.

One thing I hadn't noticed in the birth story until studying it recently was the importance of dreams. While the Bible doesn't say an angel visited Mary in a dream, Joseph had three separate occasions. In addition, the Magi were warned in a dream not to return to Herod to report they had found the new king of the Jews. In all the dreams, they were instructed in what to do, and if I can take a guess, it likely made them feel peace and comfort, reassured that everything was going to be ok. I know when I believe I am doing God's will, there is an awareness of peace and joy.

Mary and Joseph's decisions to get on board with God's plan for them was the starting point. They both showed faithfulness and bravery in doing God's will. It doesn't mean it was all smooth sailing or that they handled everything exactly the way they should, but they did what they knew to do. They followed Jewish traditions of circumcision and made the pilgrimage to Jerusalem. There is the familiar story when Jesus was twelve and he stayed behind in the temple while the rest of the family headed home. When Mary and Joseph found him, he asked, "Why were you searching for me?...Didn't you know I had to be in my Father's house?" (Luke 2:49). The next verse says they didn't understand what that meant. This shows us that even though they had a very special assignment as Jesus's human parents, they were just that—human.

Fast forward several years: while at a wedding in Cana, Mary learned the host had run out of wine. She sought Jesus to get him to help this family. His response was that it wasn't his time yet. It may have come across as Jesus being rude or disrespectful to his mother, but "Jesus was reminding her it was not yet time for people to know his true identity. Her reply and her directions to the servants indicate that she understood his desire to keep his identity concealed and that she trusted his sense of timing."[1] Jesus was able to keep his identity secret by going with the servants to turn the water into wine. In this moment, Jesus balanced the commandment to honor thy mother and father with what he was called to do. We can all relate to that on some level. Our parents and mentors guide us for a certain amount of time, but then it is up to each of us to step into the role we are called to do. The part of a host not running out of wine is important as it would have brought shame onto the family. Jesus's first true miracle, which included water of all things, was to remove shame from a family. In the end, dying on the cross, Jesus took the shame of sin off all of us.

One of the ways Jesus teaches us about what his kingdom will look like is through parables. In one, a certain man was having a great feast and invited many guests. When it came time for the guests to arrive, they gave excuses for why they couldn't come: a piece of property not seen yet, five yokes of oxen to break in, and being newly married. These reasons equated to "I don't want to come." The piece of ground can be interpreted as the world, the oxen as wealth or status, and the wife as either sensual pleasures or love of family over God.[2] The servants were then told to go get anyone off the streets to come and enjoy the feast. In this parable, we can infer that God is the host and Jesus is the servant. Jesus is still seeking and inviting all who are willing to get on board with him until all the seats are full. While Jesus's first miracle was taking shame away from one family, the true miracle is how he invites each of us into his kingdom.

When you hear about the invitation to accept Jesus, you may hear him say, "For my yoke is easy and my burden is light" (Matthew 11:30). This has been interpreted as things are easier with Jesus by your side. I don't disagree with this; however, it's not the full picture. Even Jesus's own family did not understand the full picture. They thought he was talking crazy and wanted to take him away. When Jesus was pressed about who his family was, he chose the family of God. We may be pressed as we walk further in our faith journey to remain yoked to God. For example, we might continue to struggle with a physical or mental health diagnosis. When I was asked recently if my third book would be about my ongoing mental health struggles, I responded, "What else would you want to know?" My friend Terry responded, "That progress is slow, and you can't do it on your own." There are good and bad seasons in all areas of our lives, including mentally and spiritually. Even though I know to "cast all [my] anxiety on him because he cares for [me]" (1 Peter 5:7), there are some moments when it is still a struggle. I choose to share about my struggles so others know it's okay to not be okay. The other lesson is you can't do it alone. If you have Jesus, he will help you carry any burden. But don't be afraid to seek the help you need to process your experiences. There is no shame in that.

The invitation to get on board with Jesus is extended to all of us. The challenge is not to let the excuses of worldly goals take precedence over following God's will. It can be hard to stay faithful, but I have faith we can do it with God's help. It starts with saying yes.

REFLECTION QUESTIONS:

1. *What was a challenging get-on-board moment? How did you show faithfulness by saying yes?*

2. *What excuses have you made not to seek God first in a situation or relationship?*

Act of Faithfulness: If you haven't accepted Jesus as your Savior, now is the time to get on board. If you have already made this declaration, recommit to getting on board with God today.

Song: "Promises"
by Maverick City Music

(1.)   *NIV Quest Study Bible*, Grand Rapids, MI: Zondervan, 2001, p. 1570.

(2.)   Carl Trost, Freedom Calvary, sermon, Pueblo, Colorado, January 26, 2025.

2

SHIPSHAPE

In the beginning God created the heavens and the earth.
Now the earth was formless and empty, darkness was
over the surface of the deep, and the Spirit of God
was hovering over the waters.

(Genesis 1:1–2)

WATER. WHAT AN AMAZING and complex creation if you stop to think about it. But that was only a part of what God created out of chaos. God's family started during those first few days of creation as well. God first shaped us, and we continue to be shaped through our experiences. We are chosen vessels to help build up his family through the church and in the world.

The start of any new adventure, including our faith journey, can feel muddled, chaotic, and disarrayed. If you look back at the Scripture above, you see chaotic darkness in the beginning as well. Little by little, God put together what we know as the heavens and the earth. Or instead of "put together," you could say he made it "shipshape." The definition of shipshape is "characterized by order and neatness."[3] At the end of each day during creation, God saw that it was good.

On the sixth day, God created mankind in his image, the beginning of his family. At the end of that day, he not only saw that it was good, but said that it was very good. In chapter two of Genesis, "God formed a man from the dust of the ground and breathed into his nostrils the breath of life" (v. 2:7). He created Adam (man) to take care of the earth. But a dilemma arose for God in Genesis 2:18. He said, "It is not good for the man to be alone. I will make a helper suitable for him." God brought all the animals to Adam, and while Adam gave them all names, there wasn't a suitable helper. God's solution was to create Eve (woman). In one of my Bible studies, someone observed that God solved man's first problem: loneliness. We aren't meant to be on our journey alone. Sometimes it may feel like we don't have a friend in this world, but we do. Thankfully, God is and will be with us faithfully in all our moments. He knew us before we were even born and knows all our days on this earth. And he still chooses us to be his own. Take a second to take that in.

Before a ship is sent out, there is a tradition of christening her, which includes naming her, breaking a bottle on the ship's bow, and giving her a blessing. "The history of ship christening dates back to ancient times when sailors and seafarers believed that ships had their own spirits and person-alities. They believed that if a ship was not properly named and blessed, it would not be able to navigate the seas safely."[4] If that sounds familiar, it should. As a new believer, we are called to be christened, or baptized, into our new family of believers and given a new identity in Christ. The breaking of the champagne bottle was an adaptation from the original tradition of pouring a drop of blood from a sacrificed animal onto the ship's bow. Jesus poured out his own sacrificial blood so we would all be able to join his family. The last step before a ship is sent out is the blessing for safe travels. On our faith journey, this can include a prayer over us when we first accept Jesus. We may also receive a blessing prayer as we accept a new role in our church or step into our calling. The beginning of our walk with Jesus is just the start of showing our faithfulness.

There are both good and challenging experiences that shape us in our faith journey. One of my challenging experiences was when I was verbally bullied by a few classmates in middle school. I then learned that I wasn't the only one being bullied. God showed us how we could draw strength from one another during this shared mistreatment. We decided to write a letter together to those in authority, and a meeting was held for us to face the issue head on. I do believe we were heard as the boys apologized and stopped the bullying, at least that I am aware of. It was empowering to speak up. This experience showed me that while it is not easy to put myself out there, it is important to use my voice when something is not okay.

We are all uniquely created, so it is inevitable that we won't get along with everyone we encounter. Years ago, I remember hearing Pastor David Chambers tell us there are people out there who frustrate the devil out of us. These people can include family, friends, church members, or coworkers. We can learn something from our experiences with them as well, which also shape us. First, we can learn the power of forgiveness, even if there is no apology or acknowledgement of pain by the other person. Likewise, they can teach us ways we want to be treated and how we want to treat others. Thankfully, God uses these shaping experiences to make us more into his image, if we allow him to.

One of the last things Jesus told his disciples to do was the Great Commission. "Therefore go and make disciples of all nations, baptizing them in the name of the Father and of the Son and of the Holy Spirit, and teaching them to obey everything I have commanded you. And surely I am with you always, to the very end of the age" (Matthew 28:19–20). The apostles and first believers started telling others about Jesus in the temple before they were expelled. They then began gathering in homes and, eventually, in what we would recognize as church buildings. "The structure of many early churches even reflected this nautical imagery. The main body of a church building, called the 'nave' (from the Latin navis, meaning ship), emphasizes that the Church is a vessel carrying the faithful toward salvation."[5] What a great image for the Church. We are all our own individual vessels, but we are stronger when we come together.

The Great Commission calls all of us to go and make disciples, not denominations. We are all on the same ship, Jesus's ship. Unfortunately, many divisions have been created within the church. Because of my writing journey, I have had the privilege of meeting people in several denominations who I would not have otherwise. We can be creatures of habit, staying with what is familiar because it feels safe. Staying on shore when the ship was meant to sail. What has fascinated me is how our stories can be so similar, even if we have a different style of worship. When Jesus is our focus, we are all traveling together.

When someone thinks of church, it shouldn't be limited to a worship service on Sunday morning. We are called to be the Church, not just attend one. It includes Bible study, serving the lost, and spending time with other believers. Growing up, I was involved in my church's youth group. It was a community that not only helped me shape my faith, but it is also where I began my involvement in leadership. Each experience has led me to the next, and I am constantly learning how to better lead people to seek Jesus.

"Worshippers never leave church...we carry our sanctuary with us wherever we go."[6] This means we take church outside into the world. We are all called to be the Church in every environment we are in—home, work, the community we live in. God created and is molding us, as it says in Isaiah 64:8: "Yet you, LORD, are our Father. We are the clay, you are the potter; we are all the work of your hand." Stay open to being shaped by God.

REFLECTION QUESTIONS:

1. *What is a challenging experience that shaped you?*

2. *How can you be a vessel for showing God's love with others?*

Read the creation story.
Then thank God for bringing order in your life.

Song: "a lil Church"

by TobyMac

(3.)   Vocabulary.com, s.v. "shipshape (adj)," Accessed November 29, 2025,
       https://www.vocabulary.com/dictionary/shipshape.

(4.)   "What is Ship Christening: Good Luck and Safe Travels?" Coeur Custom,
       Accessed February 22, 2025, https://www.coeurcustoms.com/uncatego-
       rized/what-is-ship-christening-good-luck-and-safe-travels/.

(5.)   Father Joe Connelly. "The Church as a Ship: A Timeless Image of Sal-
       vation," Guardian Angels Catholic Church, Accessed February 21, 2025,
       https://www.guardian-angels.org/guardian-angels-news/the-church-as-a-
       ship-a-timeless-image-of-salvation/.

(6.)   Bryan Kelsen, "Worshippers never leave the church," Facebook,
       September 2, 2025, https://www.facebook.com/bryan.kelsen.5/posts/
       pfbid02Zd9rGVbeP3AWJLgpQYn39WqgEz6vmVyR84vpS3GT5du94q
       HSdWA2MxxP1jmXwttjl

3

WHAT IS YOUR TRUE NORTH?

Gideon replied, "If now I have found favor in your eyes,
give me a sign that it is really you talking to me."

(Judges 6:17)

ONCE YOU GET ON BOARD, you begin navigating on your faith journey. God first sets our compass to face true north, which is him. This compass will guide us through our lives. It can be tempting to not follow the path he wants, but to take over the steering for our lives instead. Above all, God wants us to trust and be faithful on the path he has set for us.

The story of Jonah famously depicted someone ignoring God's will and steering their own life. God called him to go preach against the Ninevites for their wickedness. "But Jonah ran away from the LORD and headed for Tarshish" (Jonah

1:3). Instead of following God's direction, Jonah ran as fast as he could in the opposite direction. God didn't lay out the purpose of his instruction. He simply wanted Jonah to obey. Can you relate? We may not understand why God is leading us in a certain direction, but we are called to trust him. Our willingness to go where God is directing us shows our faithfulness.

Following his own path, Jonah got on a boat. Once they set out, the winds picked up, and there was a violent storm. The other people on the boat started praying to their gods, but the storm continued. They cast lots, which was a way for them to decide who was responsible for the storm. It fell on Jonah, so they asked him about his God. He admitted he was running away; therefore, he offered to be thrown overboard. Once he was in the water, the storm calmed. What I hadn't noticed before was how the other people then feared God and offered a sacrifice and made vows. God turned people who were worshipping other gods to him. God can turn one person's testing into someone else's saving moment.

The infamous part of Jonah's story was when a huge fish swallowed him. He remained there for three days and three nights. Jonah prayed a prayer of thankfulness which began: "In my distress I called to the LORD, and he answered me. From deep in the realm of the dead I called for help, and you listened to my cry" (Jonah 2:2). I can relate to that prayer, and hopefully, you do too. It shows God listens and responds to our cries. Even though Jonah was thankful for being res-cued, it didn't mean he was excused from doing what God told him to do. He still had to go to Ninevah.

I wonder if Jonah's experience changed how he approached this command. He did go and warn the Ninevites to repent or their city would be destroyed. The people, including the king, listened and repented. But, as Jonah saw their repentance, he grew angry. Even though he obeyed God's direction, he didn't want the people to be rescued. Yes, you can say that Jonah was faithful in fulfilling his call, but his heart wasn't open to seeing God's love for all people. It can be tempting for us to view a certain group of people or individuals who have hurt us as ones who don't deserve love. But God is faithful, even if we aren't. God wants us not to just be faithful, but to also truly believe in what we are being called to do.

Does God pursue those who run? That is one of the ques-tions that comes up in this story. The answer is yes, even if it may not appear that way. In all situations, he will use our experiences for our good. This is true in many stories of the Bible, including that of the prodigal son. The son was allowed to leave, to go in his own direction. But then he saw his errors and decided to turn back. Sometimes, as I have learned, we may need to take time away from a situation or place to find peace, heal, or gain a new perspective. And then

God may steer us back, but the key is to trust in where he is guiding us. God will reset our compass when we are willing.

The story of Gideon has some similarities to Jonah's story. Jonah and Gideon both showed frustration with God's directions. Gideon was more direct from the beginning, questioning why all the suffering was happening, even feeling like God had abandoned his chosen people. What I can appreciate is the angel didn't condemn Gideon for what he was feeling. Instead, the angel said "go," but it included a word of comfort: "I will be with you" (Judges 6:16). Because of his lack of trust, Gideon asked for a sign of confirmation through an offering, which the angel consumed by fire. When Gideon saw this, he realized this was an angel of the LORD. We might think having an angel appear to us would be enough to believe. However, if we are honest, we may not be as trusting as we would hope. Even though God is guiding our steps, we must be willing to be led. Thankfully, God understands, is patient with us, and puts signs out for us all the time. Our part is to stay open to seeing them, even if they are subtle.

Gideon continued to request signs from God as he was called to save Israel from the Midianites. Gideon was instructed to tear down the altar of Baal and Asherah poles and replace them with an altar built for God. Once those tasks were completed, Gideon then made his next request, which came in two parts. He put out a fleece and gave specific instructions of what he expected if it was God's will for him to save Israel from the Midianites twice. Isn't it interesting he wanted proof more than once?

"Some Christians use the phrase 'putting out a fleece' to express their desire to know exactly what God's will is for them. Putting out a fleece often describes a specific action that tests God's approval or disapproval."[7] I would like to have obvious signs from God; however, the sign he sends is most often felt as a quiet peace and calm in my heart. When it is not what God wants for me, or I am listening to lies from the devil, I am more anxious, confused, doubting myself, and letting things like jealousy and resentment take over. It can be a fight in my mind to get my focus back on God and facing true north. This is a work in progress, and all we can do is our best to keep focused on God every day.

With those confirmations fresh in his mind, Gideon faced his assignment head on. He started out with thirty-two thousand men, then God told him he had too many. After multiple instructions to downsize, Gideon went into the battle with three hundred men. Why only that many? So they would be able to say God was the reason for the victory, not the size of their army. One of my favorite battle stories was what happened next. They surrounded the enemy's camp at night, and when the time was right, they blew trumpets and broke clay jars. In the chaos and confusion, the enemy turned on each other, and Israel was able to get the victory. Similarly, we can face any challenge with God's guidance.

Most of us today can't relate to being called onto an actual battlefield, but we can question where our lives are heading. One familiar story told around Christmas time is *A Christmas Carol*. Ebenezer Scrooge is visited by his Past, Present, and Future ghosts to help him to change his projected course. A few years ago, when I was struggling with writer's block, I asked my pastor (Scott) to give me some random topics as fun writing prompts. One of his assignments was, "Which ghost would I want to have visit me?" As I thought through my answer and began writing, I ruled out Past, then Present, and assumed I would choose Future. But the more I thought about it, the more it made me leery. It made sense to be anxious about all the possible bad things that could happen. But I was just as anxious thinking about the possible good things that were to come in my life. So, I ended up choosing none of them. My pastor told me I introduced a new ghost: Ghost of Anxiety. While we would like to know that everything turns out okay, this is where we need to remind ourselves that God is always in control.

I can understand why both Jonah and Gideon wanted full and clear directions. But sometimes, even after we are challenged, the reason for the instruction still may not be clear or make sense. But as it says in Romans 8:28, "And we know that in all things God works for the good of those who love him, who have been called according to his purpose." Trust God's guidance, and you won't be steered wrong.

REFLECTION QUESTIONS:

1. *Is there a time when you know you were running away from where God was calling you? If so, how did you correct course?*

2. *Were you able to see the signs of where God was leading you, even if it was while looking back?*

Go outside at night, face north, and look up at the sky. Take a few deep breaths. Know God will be there to guide you.

Song: "Next to Me"

by Jordan Feliz

(7.) *NIV Quest Study Bible*, Grand Rapids, MI: Zondervan, 2001, p. 355.

4

ANCHORS OF LOVE

"So in everything do to others what you would have them do to you, for this sums up the Law and the Prophets."

(Matthew 7:12)

BESIDES THE NAVIGATIONAL GUIDE, it's important to have anchors on board. Merriam Webster defines an anchor as "a device usually of metal attached to a ship or boat by a cable and cast overboard to hold it in a particular place...; a reliable or principal support."[8] Anchors are used both while in port and while out at sea. We have been given anchors of love through the Law and the Prophets, which Jesus fulfilled. We are challenged to keep those anchors firmly secured in our lives.

The first anchor, the Law given to Moses, included the Ten Commandments. But first, let me set the scene. God's people were enslaved in Egypt under Pharoah's rule. Pharoah was afraid that as the Israelites kept increasing, they would revolt. He ordered all the baby boys to be murdered. Except Moses's mother cleverly put him in a basket into the water for Pharoah's daughter to discover. That was Moses's first of many God moments with water. After seeing an Egyptian beating a Hebrew, Moses killed the Egyptian and fled, stopping at a well. He met his future wife at that well—a second water moment. Many years later, Moses was called back to Egypt to rescue his Hebrew people. He showed his human side when he responded, "Pardon your servant, Lord. I have never been eloquent, neither in the past nor since you have spoken to your servant" (Exodus 4:10). Even with his reluctance, Moses showed his faithfulness by obeying God's instructions.

Moses went and asked for the release of his people, which Pharoah denied (no surprise there!). The first of ten plagues was the plague of blood, where Moses put his staff in the Nile River and the water turned to blood—the third water moment. Pharoah refused to give in, plague after plague, until his own son was killed. Pharoah then released the Hebrew people, and they began their trek to the Promised Land. But while the Red Sea was in front of them, Pharoah regretted his decision, so he sent the Egyptians to re-enslave them. Here comes the fourth water moment: God parted the Red Sea so only his people could cross on dry land. That had to be a sight to see! Once safely across, leaving the Egyptians in the sea, the people began grumbling, begging for water. Moses prayed to God for the people, then obeyed God's instructions to get them drinkable water—the fifth water moment.

However, the grumbling continued. "The Israelites [Hebrews] said to them, 'If only we had died by the LORD's hand in Egypt! There we sat around pots of meat and ate all the food we wanted, but you have brought us out into this desert to starve this entire assembly to death'" (Exodus 16:3). This was only a couple months after they left Egypt. God then provided quail and manna, which was covered in dew. In the book of Exodus, God instructed Moses to strike a rock for more water in water moment number six. These moments of water show God's faithfulness repeatedly, even if the people didn't always behave with gratefulness for what they had.

This led to the seventh moment: God spoke to Moses in a cloud on Mount Sinai and gave him what we know as the Ten Commandments. Moses and the people were already familiar with the cloud of God, a cloud by day and a pillar of fire at night as they went through the desert. This was to show God was with them, and now they were given commandments and laws to follow as God's people. Unfortunately, in the book of Numbers, even though Moses had those seven God moments, he did not follow God's next specific instruction about getting water. He was told to speak to the rock, but instead, he struck it twice. His punishment for his lack of trust was that he wasn't allowed to step into the Promised Land. This is a reminder that even though Moses wasn't perfect, he is one of the people commended for his faith in Hebrews 11. The lesson is we need to remain faithful to the best of our ability.

The Ten Commandments have two points of focus: our relationship with God and with others. All of them show our priority of love towards God. We don't want to break one because it would break our relationship with God. Or as John Wesley said centuries ago, "Love is the end of all the commandments of God. Love is the end, the sole end, of every dispensation of God, from the beginning of the world to the consummation of all things."[9] God gave the Israelites not just the Ten Commandments, but many laws to follow as they became God's people. While we can all use structure and boundaries, sometimes those same boundaries and rules can feel like walls which are impossible to climb, including the Law. But then, if we could do it all ourselves, we would feel like we didn't need God. We can never fulfill the Law, which is why Jesus had to come.

The other anchor is the prophets, who were sent from God to warn people of harm if they didn't obey. Time and time again, while the people may have been obedient for a while, they reverted to sin, worshipping other gods and disobeying the Law. By the time Jesus came to earth, the Jewish leaders added many of their own burdensome regulations to form a higher barrier to God. They saw Jesus as a threat to their power and position, but to their surprise, Jesus didn't shy away from tearing down those barriers to God. He even said, "Do not think I have come to abolish the Law or the Prophets; I have not come to abolish them but to fulfill them" (Matthew 5:17).

Jesus came to rock the boat of people's beliefs and raise the bar of expectation in how to fully obey God. When a rich man came to Jesus inquiring what he needed to do to get eternal life, Jesus told him to follow the commandments. The rich man wanted to know which ones, as in the minimum to get a passing grade. Jesus replied with a few of the Ten Commandments, but then added, "'love your neighbor as yourself'" (Matthew 19:19). The man replied that he did all those. Jesus raised the bar by telling him that he needed to sell his treasures and follow him. That was not what the man wanted to hear, and he went away sad. While it can be perceived the man was just greedy, Jesus wanted obedience. To put God first over anything else. Like it says in the Ten Commandments, God is jealous and wants priority over everything in our lives.

I think we can all understand jealousy of other people and situations. When the Israelites began grumbling about food and water, it sounds like they were feeling sentimental about their previous situation, even when it was enslavement. It is challenging to be out of your comfort zone, even if God has called you to break free of your past. These forms of enslavement can include addiction, past sin, or even relationships that are holding you back. I can testify I have felt jealousy more intensely the past few years as I step increasingly away from certain roles and situations. But I have found when I can keep my focus forward, I can feel God's love turning my jealousy into contentment.

Even when ships are sailing, the anchors are with them, tucked in their compartments. When the ship docks or stops at a specific location, the anchors are dropped to keep the ship from drifting. We can have moments in our lives when we need to stop drifting away by seeking God. When we take our dogs for walks, we put a harness on them. It helps us be able to guide them and keep them close. One of our dogs, Shadow, enjoyed going on walks, but whenever we put on her collar and harness, she would look so sad. When we took her camping a few times, it took her a long time to let herself even sit down, let alone relax. We would feel guilty and knew she was stressed, so we would let her go inside the trailer and take off her harness. But then it would be the same routine when we needed to take her outside again. While Shadow may have wanted to drift away from the campsite, we restricted her for her protection. Sometimes we may feel like God has put restrictions on us when we read all the laws and warnings from the prophets. "Faith gives us an anchor in a raging sea, calm in the midst of chaos, vision to know right from wrong, and the courage to express it."[10]

Thankfully, as believers, we have the anchor of love through Jesus's fulfilment of the prophecies, which gives us hope. "We have this hope as an anchor for the soul, firm and secure. It enters the inner sanctuary behind the curtain, where our forerunner, Jesus, has entered on our behalf" (Hebrews 6:19–20). This can be visualized as "a ship nearing port but unable to sail into the harbor because of rough seas, thick fog or low tide. A small boat carried an anchor from the ship to the pier so the ship could hold steady or painstakingly winch its way safely through the fog and into the port. Jesus entered the harbor before us, serving as our anchor of hope to lead us into God's presence."[11] Let us keep anchored to the hope and love in Jesus.

REFLECTION QUESTIONS:

1. *How has being jealous of another person or situation pulled you away from God?*

2. *Which one of the Ten Commandments is the hardest to follow?*

Ask God to show you any areas of "enslavement"
and to set you free of them.

Song: "That's Who I Praise"

by Brandon Lake

(8.) Merriam Webster Online, s.v. "anchor (n)," Accessed August 10, 2025, https://www.merriam-webster.com/dictionary/anchor.

(9.) Travels With Wesley, "Love is the end of all the commandments of God," Facebook April 26, 2025, https://www.facebook.com/travelswithwesley/posts/pfbid0YvdPnVnb1vgPXnLFXe6Bnj8vq1ZMoVWG2d7SJgDrm WesfVHjP6mwsHc3RhDUqJl.

(10.) Russ Berrie and Company, Inc., Prayer card item #24209.

(11.) *NIV Quest Study Bible*, Grand Rapids, MI: Zondervan, 2001, p. 1793.

5

IS A STORM COMING?

"Never lose hope. Storms make people stronger and never last forever." [12]

ONE THING THAT CAPTAINS watch is the weather, as it can put the ship and those on board at risk. They can stay in port or will reroute to avoid a storm. In life, on the other hand, we can't always see a storm that is brewing until it is upon us. God will help us to be as prepared as possible ahead of time, but he will also guide us through the storms. We are called to be faithful, not just on the sunny days, but through the stormy moments as well.

When I started this outline about water and ships, one of the most obvious stories to include from the Bible was Noah and the ark. I wrote about Noah in *Building Faith*, but

I decided to take another look at the story. That is one great thing about the stories in the Bible—you glean different things each time you read them. One thing that stood out this time was how only Noah was mentioned to have God's favor and called to build the ark. Not his whole family, not a group of friends or people to organize. Noah showed faithfulness in each step of building, loading the animals, and sending the different birds to confirm dry land. Even though he was the only one called, I can't imagine he built the ark all by himself. I'm sure it took some convincing that he was meant to complete this big task. Certain tasks or even a calling can sound crazy or out in left field to other people. But the peace of God helps guide you to trust in him, and not people. This may challenge you to bigger things than you could have imagined, like Noah building an ark or you pursuing a dream.

I have always loved the covenant God made with Noah with the sign of a rainbow. God promised he would never again wipe out the entire earth with a flood. What struck me was how long it took for the water to rise feet above the highest mountains. I have seen footage of flooding in various parts of the world, and it provides just a glimpse of what it was like in Noah's time. I think it's reassuring we still see rainbows today. It feels like a Godwink, a way to feel like everything is going to be okay, especially after a storm.

Another way we can see a modern version of the Noah story is through movies like *Evan Almighty*. What I appreciate about this movie is how even though it is a comedy, there are some great moments where God speaks to the characters. In one scene, God starts talking to Evan's wife, Joan, about what the story of Noah is about, and God says, "Well, I think it's a love story about believing in each other. You know, the animals showed up in pairs. They stood by each other, side by side, just like Noah and his family."[13] Joan was questioning if God called her husband to build the ark, and God's answer in the movie was to look at the calling as an opportunity to show their love and belief in one another, including God. God showed his love for Noah by saving him, while Noah trusted God in this assignment. Experiences like building an ark can bring people closer and test their patience. We may not understand why a certain storm in our life comes rolling in, but we can look at it as an opportunity to show our faithfulness and trust in God. He will bring us through any storm, but we must be willing to ride those choppy waves.

A part of the story often overlooked is what happened after the water receded. Noah was working in a vineyard, drank too much, and was lying naked in his tent. Being naked was viewed as a form of shame. His son Ham saw him naked and told his brothers. The brothers then covered Noah up. However, because Ham had dishonored Noah, Noah cursed Ham's descendants. That's not the fairytale ending we all think of in Noah's story. This shows us how we can still mess up with worldly sin. Thankfully, as believers, we have Jesus who has covered our sins with his grace.

Jesus also showed grace when the disciples' struggled with their faith during a storm. One of my favorite stories of Jesus in a boat is when he was sleeping while a storm was brewing. I can totally picture the apostles' frustration and shock as Jesus was peacefully sleeping. I can relate as I sometimes feel like Jesus is totally unaware of my situation, oblivious to my needs. But when Jesus woke up, he said, "You of little faith, why are you so afraid?" (Matthew 8:26). Jesus then quickly rebuked the winds, the storm calmed down, and the disciples were amazed the weather obeyed him. My educated guess is they weren't expecting that response, but Jesus's question doesn't seem so off-base. The disciples had seen many miracles and listened to his teaching. However, it can be hard to feel peace or calm in a storm. We can find comfort that while the disciples didn't always show the ideal faith, Jesus still calmed their storm.

Another time the disciples were in a boat in a storm, Jesus was not with them. He had just provided food for five thousand men, not including women and children, and he told the disciples to go ahead of him. "Jesus, knowing that they intended to come and make him king by force, withdrew again to a mountain by himself" (John 6:15). As the disciples were on the boat, a sudden storm came on the Sea of

Galilee. As they looked out, they thought a ghost was walking on the water towards them. Jesus reassured them it was him and to not be afraid. This was when Peter had a moment of faithfulness to trust Jesus to walk out on the water. He did well when he kept his focus on Jesus. When Peter lost his focus and started to doubt, Jesus was right there to help him. It wasn't until Jesus joined them in the boat that the storm calmed down and they were safe. In both stories, calling out to Jesus and hearing his reassurance helped to calm the disciples and build trust that he will always be there.

When I decided to move to Denver, Colorado, for graduate school, I chose to live in an apartment by myself. One night, I was in a deep sleep during a thunderstorm. I was awakened by a clap of thunder and saw a flash of lightning at nearly the same time. I crawled out of my bed and into the hallway as an automatic response from my limbic system, triggering a fight or flight reaction. My body needed to get somewhere safe. The next thunderstorm, I could feel my heart beating faster as I was having the same emotions as that night. I had to tell myself I was safe and take some deep breaths. These are called grounding techniques, in which you refocus on the present instead of the anxiety and fear. They helped me feel calm through the storm.

When I try to describe my moments of anxiety and depression, my best description is that you feel like you are in a hurricane. For one, as the storm picks up, it can feel manageable. But as it gets stronger and keeps going, it can feel like the world is spiraling out of control. That is how my thoughts can go. I am ok, but then as moments pass, the thoughts get darker and more negative. Then, if the storm gets too loud, it's all consuming and any music or words of encouragement get drowned out. The storm feels like it will never end. They say there is an eye of the storm where it seems to be over, but then the storm hits again, sometimes even stronger. When I was deeper in my depression episode a few years ago, it felt like it was never going to end. It was challenging to have any hope that someday my mind would be calm again. I felt better for several days, like the eye of the storm, but then the storm returned more intensely. It felt like I was treading water, barely keeping my head above the waves. I was exhausted and ready to give up when, like Peter, Jesus showed me mercy. It wasn't an immediate end to that storm, but God gave me the strength to endure. The lesson is to seek God in any way you can. This includes prayer, listening to Christian songs, and reading the Bible. While it may not feel like you are seeking God in the storm, do the best you can. Take all your thoughts and emotions to God, including your doubts and fears, and turn them over to him.

These examples don't say there will not be another storm or challenge in your future. Past storms can create fear of how bad the next storm might be. Thankfully, "having God in your boat doesn't mean that you'll not face any storms. It means that no storm can sink your boat. Walk in faith and you will never walk alone."[14]

REFLECTION QUESTIONS:

1. *When was a time that God called you to do something others may have thought was crazy?*

2. *How has God helped you through a storm in your life?*

Find a Scripture to memorize to remind you that God is always with you.

Song: "Eye of the Storm"

by Ryan Stevenson

(12.) Roy T. Bennett, "Never lose hope," Goodreads, Accessed September 21, 2025, https://www.goodreads.com/quotes/7976897-never-lose-hope-storms-make-people-stronger-and-never-last.

(13.) Tom Shadyac dir., *Evan Almighty*, Universal Pictures, 2007, viewed via YouTube.

(14.) Kim Gic, "Having God in your boat," Facebook, September 21, 2025, https://www.facebook.com/kim.gic.2024/posts/pfbidopHgaTLıhoıy AtMYx5uWaiReNz3NADamGVrcY7qBAduodQuLaSv9VePSkLPaugFevl

6

WHAT DO YOU TAKE WITH YOU?

"Ships don't sink because of the water around them.
Ships sink because of the water that gets in them.
Don't let what's happening around you get inside
you and weigh you down." [15]

WHEN YOU THINK ABOUT going on a trip, you likely look at the weather report to know what clothing to take. Usually, you only have limited space, so you must be selective. While it's important to know what you're taking, you also need to assess what you need to leave behind. Unhealthy baggage we can carry includes toxic people, situations, and our own attitudes. It will take leaving those behind to take the trip of faith God has called you on.

The first example from the Bible of wanting to leave baggage behind was the woman who was bleeding for twelve years. She tried everything to find a cure, spending all her money on doctors. You can feel her desperation, as she believed just touching Jesus's clothes would heal her. Jesus was on his way to heal a dying child when he felt the power go out of him. When he asked who touched him, the disciples were quite confused, as they were likely shoulder to shoulder with many people. While it may have been scary to admit it was her, the woman stepped forward and shared her story.

Then Jesus said, "Daughter, your faith has healed you. Go in peace and be freed from your suffering" (Mark 5:34). Two things in that statement are comforting. First, he called her daughter, which is a term of endearment and shows his concern for his child. Second, she was freed from her suffering. Twelve years was a long time to be separated from others as it was custom not to get close to others while bleeding. It was considered unclean. There were many laws concerning blood and the steps you had to take to be allowed back into community. That would be manageable for a few days during a normal situation, but year after year had to have taken a toll. Additionally, others not understanding what she was going through could have made her feel even more alone. While the physical healing would have made her feel lighter, I believe it was the freedom to reconnect with the community that was the bigger release. "It would have been in her best interest— not to mention the crowd's—to tell others what had happened to her. Thus, a person timid faith became a faithful witness."[16]

Her boldness to reach for Jesus, while technically breaking the law of not touching others while ceremonially unclean, shows us how we may need to be bolder in our faith in God as well.

While the woman was able to act on her faith, my next example shows how we may be challenged to make a decision. There was a pool at Bethesda that people claimed had healing powers when the waters stirred. Whoever made it into the water first would be healed. Not surprisingly, many people with ailments stayed close by the pool for that small chance.

> *One who was there had been an invalid for thirty-eight years. When Jesus saw him lying there…he asked him, "Do you want to get well?"*
>
> *"Sir," the invalid replied, "I have no one to help me into the pool when the water is stirred…."*
>
> *Then Jesus said to him, "Get up! Pick up your mat and walk." At once the man was cured; he picked up his mat and walked* (John 5:5–9).

In this story, while Jesus knew the man was an invalid, he also did not accept his excuse of blaming others. This is confirmed when after the man was healed, he found Jesus who told him, "See, you are well again. Stop sinning or something worse may happen" (John 5:14). Sometimes, it takes a command like that to stir up our desire to make changes in our lives that we do have control over. These changes can include our thoughts, attitudes, and reactions to situations.

We would like to see those instant healings and changes happen in our own lives. I can relate to the bleeding woman, not just because I am also a woman, but because I had a fibroid cyst in my uterus, which is common. I was having worse symptoms than normal, but I was fortunate to have testing and doctors to diagnose and provide options for how to address the problem. I know it's not always a simple process to figure out what may be going on in your body and hard to stay positive when test after test is performed.

While my medical issue was straightforward, my struggles with mental health have taken many twists and turns. Like the man by the pool, I can understand the temptation to push the blame onto other people instead of admitting how my own thoughts contributed to the struggles. It can wear on you when the healing doesn't seem to come quickly. You may even hear of others being healed while you are still struggling. What we must guard against is destructive thinking turning into a stumbling block for ourselves, others, or both. "A stumbling block is an obstacle in a path that causes a person to lose balance or fall. It can be an enticement to sin, or a test from the Lord intended to reveal a person's true commitments and beliefs."[17] Jesus reinforced this idea, challenging us not to be a stumbling block to others. He used the illustration that if our hand or foot causes us to stumble, then we are to cut it off. It was a graphic way for us to understand not to let any area of our lives hinder our faith. The woman who was bleeding could have just given up, but she kept seeking. The man by the pool let his disability be his own stumbling block.

While I was working on this chapter, my husband and I decided to go on a trip up to the mountains. I found a magazine in our hotel room that had some suggestions for hikes. One that caught my eye was described as an easy three-mile roundtrip hike to Lily Pad Lake near Frisco, Colorado. I looked up how to get to the trailhead, and we were off. It became apparent in the first few minutes that this was not just a casual stroll, but closer to a moderate-level mountain hike. Our hike began around nine thousand feet, requiring us to take several breaks to catch our breath. Since it was early May, not all the snow had melted on the path. It was clear people had hiked before us, so we followed their steps in the patches of snow to the best of our ability. There was a moment, or several, in which I questioned whether we would ever get to that lake. I almost gave up. When we got to the lake, we were able to celebrate. Unfortunately, it was too early for the lily pads to bloom as the lake was iced over. But there was celebration of our faithfulness to keep pressing onward.

As we hiked up and back, I reflected on many things that can be stumbling blocks in life. On the hike, we had multiple physical things that had the potential to trip us or cause us to stumble—rocks, exposed tree roots, mud, and snow. Some of the snow was already packed down, but every now and then, a foot would sink into the fresh snow. Right before we got to the lake, there was a hole in the snow, exposing marsh and deeper water below. We were successful in how we faced this section on the way up, but I had some trouble on the way back down. I took one step, and my husband said, "No, not there," and then my next step was followed again by "No, not there." While I had been able to keep out of the deeper water before this, both my feet got a little soaked on these few steps. We celebrated again when we made it back to our car.

This adventure taught me many lessons. First, we may unknowingly be on a path that is more challenging than we had hoped. Second, we may have similar tests and trials like other people, but it is up to each of us to decide to keep going. Third, we might be the one who is stopping ourselves from pursuing our calling or dream. Or, as I relied only on my husband's directions over the marsh, we may not trust our own gut for the next step. But we also must make sure these challenges don't become excuses or distractions from the path we are meant to be on. This includes mentally, physically, and spiritually. Finally, we had greater joy making it through the challenge because we knew what it took to complete it.

All these examples show us how our faith can be tested with what baggage we choose to carry with us. It may be a physical or mental diagnosis, or situations that push us further than we ever thought they would. We may need to leave certain parts of us—including relationships, a job, a title, or expectations from others—to be able to faithfully follow

God. We will feel freer when we release those things that are slowing us down. Let that baggage go!

REFLECTION QUESTIONS:

1. *Who do you relate to more when you think of healing: the bleeding woman or disabled man?*

2. *How have you been a stumbling block for someone else or yourself?*

Ask God to show you a negative piece of "baggage" you have been holding onto. Trust God to let it go.

Song: "Even Then"

by Micah Tyler

(15.) God Winks, "Ships don't sink because of the water around them," Facebook, January 5, 2025, https://www.facebook.com/permalink.php?story_fbid=pfbidowGdiTavvMGMkPhRhQihbEVrMkA4SwzjaMjxGVSetuqJCyewoUhQpzfZSuc5EQ3szl&id=100064538090352.

(16.) *NIV Quest Study Bible*, Grand Rapids, MI: Zondervan, 2001, p. 1483.

(17.) *NIV Quest Study Bible*, Grand Rapids, MI: Zondervan, 2001, p. 1220.

PART TWO

THE SHIPS
of our
FAITH JOURNEY

7

MEMBERSHIP DUES

*For he chose us in him before the creation of the world to be
holy and blameless in his sight. In love he predestined us for
adoption to sonship through Jesus Christ, in accordance with
his pleasure and will—to the praise of his glorious grace,
which he has freely given us in the One he loves.*

(Ephesians 1:4–6)

WHEN I LOOKED UP membership in the online dictionary,
Merriam-Webster gave the general definition of being part
of a group. But it also suggested we compare membership
with inclusion.[18] This is what membership truly is: being for-
mally included in a group, church, or organization. God has
called each one of us to be identified in his family through
adoption. The definition which best describes this adoption
process is "the act or process of giving official acceptance."[19]

The question to all of us is: Will we be faithful in putting God first over human relationships? Ultimately, how we choose to use words like membership, inclusion, identity, and adoption makes a difference in how we view ourselves in the world.

While I was preparing for this chapter, I was reminded of the story of Hannah, the mother of Samuel. The story begins with the picture of a man with two wives: Peninnah, who had children, and childless Hannah. Not having children in that time was seen as God not showing favor to the woman, a sign of disgrace. While Hannah endured her rival's provocations, she chose to faithfully seek God. She prayed that if God were to give her a son, she would give him to the Lord. One of the priests, Eli, saw her praying and told her God would give her what she wanted. It doesn't say how long it was between the time she prayed and gave birth. However, Hannah showed her faithfulness and had joy and hope before she knew she was pregnant. The lesson is to remain faithful while waiting. It may take changing our attitude towards the situation before God grants us what we want, if it is God's will.

Hannah followed through with her end of the deal to give her son to the Lord. "She named him Samuel, saying 'Because I asked the LORD for him'" (1 Samuel 1:20). Hannah's identity went from one of shame to one filled with God's grace because of her faithfulness.

Hannah continued to make her annual sacrifices, and Eli prayed over Hannah and her husband, Elkanah, saying, "May the LORD give you children by this woman to take the place of the one she prayed for and gave to the LORD" (1 Samuel 2:20). She did have more children, and while she isn't mentioned again, her sacrifice had a kingdom-sized impact. Eli raised Samuel, who became a prophet of the Lord. While we cannot know for sure, Samuel could have felt abandoned by his parents. Instead, he was able to focus on faithfully serving God, even anointing the first two kings of Israel.

Showing where our loyalty lies is a key to being included in a group. Some organizations, like political groups, seem to focus on putting the other side down. On the other hand, in the Bible, when we read about showing loyalty to God over other gods or idols, the focus is on God and his goodness. We are all tested to show where our loyalty lies—in God or the world. Daniel's story showed his loyalty, his membership, was in God's family. He was one of the exiles taken from Israel to Babylon and served under multiple kings. While he was given a new name in Babylon, his loyalty remained to God. He was able to interpret the kings' dreams and gained respect. That respect grew into jealousy from his peers.

When King Darius came into power, he was talked into issuing an edict that required the people to only pray to him and no other gods for the next thirty days. The consequence for disobeying was being thrown into a den of lions.

Not surprisingly, Daniel continued his daily prayers to God, and the other men tattled on him. While the king was upset over the punishment dictated by the edict, he needed to follow through. So, Daniel spent the night in the lions' den with the entrance sealed. His response in the morning was "My God sent his angel, and he shut the mouths of the lions. They have not hurt me, because I was found innocent in his sight. Nor have I ever done any wrong before you, Your Majesty" (Daniel 6:22). The lesson we can learn is while others may try to diminish your light and faith, God sees your loyalty. It may cause you pain while on earth, but the blessings that will come are everlasting. The book of Daniel also prophesies what is to come, including God's everlasting kingdom of believers.

When I read a Scripture about being adopted into God's family, it hits me in a different way than a lot of people. I will preface this story with knowing not everyone may understand my specific experience. Growing up, while I was raised by my biological family, there were many occasions they told me I was adopted and belonged to the family next door. When I had the courage to ask whether this was true, I was told they were just joking. I know a lot of families use that excuse when something like that is said. But to me, it wasn't funny. It made me question where I belonged, and it cultivated a fear of abandonment.

One response I got more recently was, "Wouldn't being told you were adopted make you feel more wanted?" For children who are adopted, they could interpret their biological parents as having rejected them. While I wasn't adopted, I carry emotional scars of rejection. I have also carried feelings of shame and embarrassment because I wondered how I could have believed them, which made me want to keep this part of my journey a secret. But I feel God is calling me now to be vulnerable and courageous because this can make a difference for the people who read this. Even if you can't relate to this story, you may have had times of feeling rejected, alone, or questioning your membership and identity in your community. Thankfully, I have been shown and can share how God's love is eternal. He makes us feel wanted, and he will never abandon us.

In situations like this, I have learned that words matter. What we say and how we handle situations matter. While saying I was adopted may have been brushed aside, the impact of these words had lasting effects. On the other hand, the words we use can also deeply touch our hearts, where we know and feel we are loved. One prayer my pastor said over me recently meant so much to me as I truly felt like Jesus was saying these words to me. In part, he said, "I was a child of God, and no matter if people disappoint me, God loves me." While I can sit and wish things in my past weren't there, they have shaped me into who I am today. I have put time into healing my wounds, wounds which will continue to heal. This healing includes recognizing that while there was no malicious intent in their words, they still hurt me. God helped me to forgive them. While the process of working through these wounds has felt like my heart has shattered repeatedly, God has been healing them with his love.

While these lessons in membership can feel intense, God also showed me an everyday example. I like to help with yardwork, including trimming bushes. However, I sometimes cut the extension cord to the electric hedge trimmer. I get going on my task, and without warning, it stops working. It is then when I realize that the cord is severed. I must admit to my husband that, yes, I did it again. He can then hopefully repair it with some electrical tape. Relationships with other people will need times of repair, or in certain circumstances, the ties need to be cut off. On the other hand, I am grateful God will not sever our relationship, even if it seems beyond repair. He may need to help heal our broken pieces, but it is up to us to accept his extension of grace and mercy.

Feel assured that no matter what your family or community looks like, as a believer, you are identified as a member of God's family, as it says, "'I will be a Father to you, and you will be my sons and daughters, says the Lord Almighty'" (2 Corinthians 6:18). Unlike other memberships, being a believer doesn't cost us any money. The admission fee was paid by Christ, and all we need to do is say yes.

REFLECTION QUESTIONS:

1. *How did you handle a time of testing? What did you learn?*

2. *What words have had a positive impact on you?*

Listen to the words in the song "The Truth"
and know you are a child of God.

Song: "The Truth"

by Megan Woods

(18.) Merriam Webster Online, s.v. "membership (n)," Accessed September 13, 2025, https://www.merriam-webster.com/dictionary/membership.

(19.) Merriam Webster Online, s.v. "adoption (n)," Accessed September 14, 2025, https://www.merriam-webster.com/dictionary/adoption.

8

FOLLOW THE LEADER

"Be careful who you let on your ship,
because some people will sink the whole ship
just because they can't be the captain." [20]

MANY SAY THEY DON'T want to be a leader; instead, they would rather follow someone else. Jesus gave us the best example of this when he repeatedly told people, "Follow me." Yet, we are all called to be leaders in different areas of our lives: in our families, at our workplaces, and in our churches. Recognizing when our faithfulness must take precedence over a title will be a challenge throughout our lives. In all positions of leadership, our obedience to God's will is our best choice. We are all called to be leaders, as we are called to lead other people to Jesus.

The first example of leadership is John the Baptist. He was Jesus's cousin who leapt in the womb when Jesus was nearby. John's ministry started a few years before Jesus's baptism. The Gospel of Mark jumps right into this story about a messenger coming to prepare the way for the Lord. John preached "a baptism of repentance for the forgiveness of sins" (Mark 1:4). People flocked to him, confessing their sins, and were baptized. The gospel writers reference Isaiah 40, in which Luke quotes the longest version and includes verses 4–5, which in part says, "The crooked roads shall become straight, the rough ways smooth. And all the people will see God's salvation" (Luke 3:5–6). Many Jews had to be excited about a new prophet after nearly four hundred years of silence, especially since John was dressed similarly to Elijah and other prophets. However, along with the excitement came condemnation from the Pharisees and Sadducees, exposing their hypocrisy and lack of true repentance.

The turning point in John's life was when Jesus came to him to be baptized. John was baptizing people as a form of repentance; however, he would tell the people someone greater was coming after him. When Jesus stepped into the public, John knew his own role of leadership would lessen as he said, "He must become greater; I must become less" (John 3:30). While John knew this was the plan all along and was faithful in his role, it had to have come with mixed emotions. His own followers seemed torn between the two men. John also showed his human side when, while in prison, he sent people to Jesus to question if Jesus was the Messiah. John knew the Scriptures, yet he needed reassurance that he was correct. Jesus answered by telling them to report all the miracles they had seen. While Jesus didn't appear to be fulfilling what the Jewish people thought a Messiah would be like, he was actually exceeding those expectations. We also have to be careful not to judge a leader's actions by what we believe they should do.

Following Jesus is both easier and harder the more you step out in faith. The role of a leader comes with sacrifices, even death. John the Baptist spoke out against Herod, who married his brother's wife, which landed him in jail. John's words upset Herod's new wife; therefore, she and her daughter concocted a plan to have John beheaded. When one steps up to a leadership position, the criticism and attacks are unfortunately part of the package. I once heard when things go wrong, the blame goes to the leader; however, when things go right, it is a team effort. Criticism can wear a leader down, but it is a good test of faithfulness to keep going despite frustrations that arise. While sacrifices and painful moments are a part of leadership, we must be on guard to not let those dominate our thoughts. Thankfully, we have the best example in Jesus of how to handle situations. Jesus often went away to pray, knew the Scriptures, and chose his words wisely. Most importantly, he was obedient to God's will, not his own.

Sometimes, being a leader means waiting to be chosen. That example was best shown in Barsabbas. After Judas Iscariot's death, the other apostles wanted to replace him. There were two men nominated: Joseph called Barsabbas and Matthias. They used the practice of casting lots because they believed it was God indicating the right choice. The lot fell to Matthias. But I wonder what Barsabbas was feeling. "It's one thing for a person to tell you 'no,' but for God to say 'no' carries much more weight.... He proved his true character in how he reacted to *not* being chosen—that's integrity."[21] The next time we hear about Barsabbas is when he was chosen as one of the leaders in Antioch. This indicates Barsabbas continued to be a leader, even if he wasn't one of the Twelve. Just because you're not the pastor or musician doesn't mean you can't be a leader in a prayer group or serve the homeless. Leadership comes in many forms, and we need to be open to where the Holy Spirit wants and equips us to lead.

When I quit my job scheduling caregivers, I wanted and needed to not be a leader. I got a job as a receptionist in a medical office for a better work/life balance. It was a relief not to be in charge at my job. As time went on and I learned more about the billing side, I was able to help in more aspects of the business. While I had no plans to move up in the company, God did. He was preparing me for some big changes. When the office manager decided to retire, the job was presented to me. I had recently stepped down from my leadership role as worship chair at church due to burnout. Being a people pleaser, I felt I needed to step up at work. My leadership focus and sense of purpose turned to my job. Sometimes we can make decisions based on fueling our egos over God's will. Whatever the reasons I had, it was what both the company and I needed.

After our second move of office locations, I thought things would settle down. Nope. Onto a bigger change: The company went through a merger. This was a complete overhaul of furniture, electronics, scanning all our paper charts, and learning a whole new computer system. I was also continuing to take care of the "old" company's things. I still don't totally know how I balanced that, but every day, we were able to check things off our list. It was quite challenging to try to help the staff with questions as I was learning the new electronic health record system along with them. Also, because I had to split my time between the companies, I felt a step behind all the staff as they put all their attention on only one job. What I find fascinating was I was on fire writing my second book throughout the several months the merger was happening. But it was what grounded me and helped to pull me through it. My time writing connected me more to God.

As the months went on and the need for assisting with all the logistics lessened, there was a plan for me to move more into the billing side. Unfortunately, there was turnover in our front desk position so that was my priority for several months. Once we were fully staffed at our location, it was agreed that my only focus would be on billing, taking the manager role off my plate. While it felt like I had failed in my leadership role, I had to admit that it was overwhelming. Every shift in my role at this job pushed me to trust that I was where I needed to be at that time. In each of the work examples, it took courage to accept the positions given, but also when those positions changed.

Leadership can be hard, frustrating, and push you to your limits. It comes in many shapes and sizes and may change over time, requiring a lot of flexibility. Leadership can be a test of your faith to stay the course over jumping ship. What we can be assured of is God will be there, guiding us as we lead others.

REFLECTION QUESTIONS:

1. *How does faithfulness apply to leadership?*

2. *What area of your life can you step up more as a leader?*

Send a thank you card to a leader in your life
(examples: pastor, boss, someone you admire as a leader).
Tell them how you appreciate what they do.

Song: "Place in This World"

by Michael W. Smith

(20.) Nature global, "A wise man once said," Facebook, July 29, 2025, https://
www.facebook.com/permalink.php?story_fbid=pfbid0385gYpMm
GpGVfvnWgVrHayezcDG10JPSPWeQxG1hT85msULVABLbsJ
CwB769VA8Qul&id=100083323335810.

(21.) Peter DeHaan, "Who Is Barsabbas?" Peter DeHaan, February 24, 2021,
https://www.peterdehaan.com/bible/who-is-barsabbas/.

9

PLANTING APOSTLES

PLANTING SEEDS. UNLIKE THE quote above, the men known to us as the apostles had their lives completely changed in an instant. The definition of apostle, *apóstolos* in Greek, means "one who is sent out."[23] The apostles went from their ordinary lives to seeing miracles, casting out demons, and seeing the risen Son of God. Their faith started as a small seed, but it transformed into their eternal salvation. Salvation was not just limited to the apostles but, through generations spreading the good news, has led to ours as well.

The apostles included fishermen, a tax collector, and a zealot. We don't have an account of each of the Twelve being called, but it had to have been life changing for each of them. To drop their livelihood to follow Jesus was just the first test of their faith. For one example, Simon (Peter) had been out fishing all night with his crew when Jesus showed up and started preaching in one of their boats. When Jesus finished, he told Simon to go out to fish again. Simon, tired and frustrated with their lack of success so far, complied with the request. To his surprise, their nets began overflowing with fish to the point they needed a second boat to help them. Both boats then became so full of fish that they started to sink. That's a lot of fish! "When Simon Peter saw this, he fell at Jesus' knees and said, 'Go away from me, Lord; I am a sinful man'" (Luke 5:8). Jesus tells them not to be afraid, and he and his fishing partners would now be fishing for men. The men left everything they knew and followed Jesus.

The seeds of their willingness to drop everything for Jesus had to have been planted years before. They had heard the stories from what we know as the Old Testament and the prophecies about the Messiah. Those seeds of knowledge and understanding were growing, preparing them to make this decision to say yes. When Jesus called Matthew, he was having a meal with tax collectors and sinners. The Pharisees were appalled at this, but Jesus didn't ask the expected people to follow him. "'It is not the healthy who need a doctor, but the sick. I have not come to call the righteous, but sinners'" (Mark 2:17). Jesus showed his ministry was going to look different than what people had set in their minds.

The apostles saw many miracles, and despite that, it seemed like they still didn't get it. The apostles fought over who was going to be the greatest, and the mom of two disciples asked Jesus for favored seats for her sons. Even if something is right in front of you, you can miss it if you're not looking. Jesus chose to love them, despite their lack of understanding and weaknesses. Jesus shows us that same love, even with our shortcomings.

Jesus displayed sacrificial love during what we call Holy week, starting with the triumphal entry into Jerusalem. People waved branches and yelled, "Hosanna," meaning "save us." While Jesus and his apostles made their way into Jerusalem, they also likely saw people being crucified on crosses. The Roman Empire displayed those who rebelled in these public executions to keep their subjects in line. Crucifixion usually took days, not hours, of slowly losing the ability to breathe. For Jesus to know he would suffer that same death, but chose to go anyway to save us all, is quite powerful. Jesus showed us how being faithful can lead us to painful, brutal, and heart-wrenching experiences. But, if we can do God's will despite our own suffering, it can have an everlasting effect.

Jesus also knew his apostles would all fall away as his death was imminent. It took hearing about Jesus's rising from the dead and then seeing him themselves for them to start to understand what they had just experienced. In the book of John, with uncertainty of what to do next, many disciples were found back on the lake, fishing. A mysterious person tells them to put the nets on the other side, and when the fish start filling the nets, they're able to see that the mysterious person was Jesus. It appears to be a time of doing what was familiar, maybe to help them process all that had happened. I can understand that. It was a place of comfort after a stressful time. Maybe that's why there was fifty days between Jesus's resurrection and Pentecost, when the apostles were officially sent off to spread the good news. They needed that time to grow a little, or maybe a lot, stronger spiritually.

Jesus said, "The Kingdom of heaven is like a mustard seed, which a man took and planted in his field. Though it's the smallest of all seeds, yet when it grows, it is the largest of garden plants and becomes a tree, so that the birds come and perch in its branches" (Matthew 13:31–32). Something as small as a seed can grow into a tree when given the right nutrients. In the natural world, this includes proper soil, water, sun, and removing the weeds. Spiritually, the nutrients include watering our faith with knowledge of the Bible. Planted in us are the fruit of the Spirit and our gifts. We need to regularly cultivate our faith through time in prayer.

Growth is seen when we turn what we have learned into serving others with those gifts.

While on a Zoom meeting with fellow believers recently, I was asked a tough question: How can one go from faith as small as a mustard seed to the apostles' level of faith? I don't remember exactly what I said, but I know I pointed out that while we can put the apostles on pedestals, even they struggled at times in their faith. There is only one who not only had perfect faith, but the capacity for it—Jesus. Like in gardening, it takes persistence and effort for faith to grow. When we planted our garden one year, I joked with my husband about harvesting the day after we put the seeds in. Unfortunately, plants don't grow overnight. It's the same with our faith. We want to understand everything right away. I know when I have studied a certain Scripture again, something new is revealed or someone else's interpretation helps me see it in a new way. Those moments help my faith grow a little more.

When you plant a garden, you must know which plants can or can't be near each other. If you put two vegetables that both need a lot of water, like cucumbers and zucchini, together, they will fight over that resource. It can be like that if all people have the same gift, which can lead to competition and jealousy. That may be why Jesus chose people with different strengths. When a tree is blooming, many different animals can benefit: birds can make nests, the fruit can feed little creatures, and other animals can enjoy the shade. The tree can live on if used for paper. While a tree was growing to ultimately become this book (unless you're reading the ebook), God planted the seed of writing in me. Like when the apostles immediately followed Jesus, the Holy Spirit told me now is the time to pursue writing. God will show us when it is time to bear the fruit he has planted in us and share our gifts with others.

Even though the apostles lived over two thousand years ago, we are benefiting from their plantings. While we may not be called to apostleship, we are all called to be sent out, planting seeds of faith in others. Put your trust in God to water them in his time. "Sow your seed in the morning, and at evening let your hands not be idle, for you do not know which will succeed, whether this or that, or whether both will do equally well" (Ecclesiastes 11:6). Never doubt the smallness of a seed. It can bloom into something beautiful.

REFLECTION QUESTIONS:

1. *What seed was planted in your life years ago?*

2. *What Scripture have you found something new in which helped your faith grow?*

Plant a seed of faith in someone you meet.

Song: "Flowers"

by Samantha Ebert

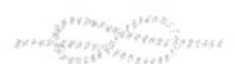

(22.) The Unraveling by Kelli Bachara, "You might not completely change someone's life," Facebook, September 22, 2021, https://www.facebook.com/ theunravelingblog/posts/pfbid0QpGcQsVCjyf8sPqBjMTkgLrvV 75zb1UAgU4w2QPQ1QBHPxHvTXcNsEwP4vDXfDbYl.

(23.) Vocabulary.com, s.v. "apostle (n)," Accessed May 17, 2025, https://www. vocabulary.com/dictionary/apostle.

10

WHAT DOES WORSHIP LOOK LIKE?

"Worship isn't just sitting in a church pew, raising your hands, and singing a few Christian songs. Worship is a lifestyle. It's seeking to honor and obey God in word, thought, and deed. It's living with a heart completely for God." [24]

WHEN ONE THINKS OF the word "worship," it's tempting to think it is limited to a church service once a week. However, as in the introductory quote, it is so much more. Expanding our definition of the word can bring us more joy, but it also can bring out other emotions. We can be drawn to worship not only in celebration, but also in moments surrounding grief. We may also be tested in our faithfulness to worship during a challenging chapter in life.

Abraham's faithfulness was tested many times in his life, starting with being told to pick up and move. He was given a promise that his descendants would become a great nation. Without having the Law and guidance of how to worship, Abraham built an altar once he made it to the land he was given. Even though he was promised offspring, he didn't immediately receive any. Instead of trusting God's promise, Abraham tried to figure out his own way to pass on this inheritance. His first plan was to create an heir through his servant, Eliezer, but God promised him it would be Abraham's own flesh and blood. In Abraham and his wife Sarah's second plan, Abraham fathered a child, Ishmael, with their slave, Hagar. Then God made the covenant with Abraham through the act of circumcision of all males. As a result, Abraham's wife, Sarah, became pregnant with their child, Issac. Abraham waited twenty-five years for this promise to come true. That is a long time to remain faithful.

Several years later, Abraham was tested again. "Then God said, 'Take your son, your only son, whom you love—Issac—and go to the region of Moriah. Sacrifice him there as a burnt offering on a mountain I will show you'" (Genesis 22:2). What an act of worship that Abraham was asked to do. The next day, Abraham set off with Issac. On the third day, Abraham told his servants, "We will worship and then we will come back to you" (Genesis 22:5). When they reached the place, Abraham built an altar, bound Issac, and put the wood on top. That is quite an image. Right before Abraham sacrificed his own son, God stepped in and provided a ram for sacrifice instead. Since God tested Abraham, we may wonder if God tests us as well. Tests of faith "help uncover our real motives, clarify our deep loyalties, eliminate deceit and nurture genuine faith."[25] Because of Abraham's faithfulness, the angel of the LORD declared blessings over Abraham. A test of faithfulness turned into a time of joy and deeper worship of God.

Sometimes times of testing can feel like a circumcision. I once heard of a comparison between God's covenants to Noah and Abraham. Abraham got what sounded like a painful experience in circumcision, while Noah got a wonderful rainbow. That doesn't sound fair to me. But we can forget all the years of faithfulness that Noah showed while building the ark. While it may look like another person is just skating by, enjoying their rainbows, we may be going through a time of deepening our faith. Whatever our time of testing looks like, such as Abraham's painful experience or Noah's completing a challenging task, it is important to continue to worship God through it all.

A time of illness or struggle can influence how we worship. Simon's mother-in-law was sick with a fever when Jesus was called to step in. "So he went to her, took her hand, and helped her up. The fever left her and she began to wait on them" (Mark 1:31). This short story has so much packed in it.

Jesus was made aware of a need and ministered to her, and she immediately started serving. When I picture this scene, one minute she was sick in bed, and the next she was making a meal. That immediate action shows me she was so grateful for her healing and that serving was her form of worship. She didn't have to go up to an altar on a distant mountain to serve. She could use her gifts right where she was.

For me, the word "worship" became distorted a few years ago. When the COVID pandemic started in 2020, our church was faced with what worship would look like when we recorded our services. Being the worship chair, I put pressure on myself to make it as close to what it would be like if people were still in the church building. Only those who experienced filming these "worship services" can understand the silence in a sanctuary that was once filled with noise. After we started meeting again in person, and even to this day, those moments of silence can still catch me during a Sunday service. It can be easy to take moments for granted, like praying the Our Father or singing together. We may not realize how precious those moments are until they are only a memory.

The intensity of that time, along with many other factors, led me to burnout in February 2022, when I just couldn't do it anymore. Even the word "worship" felt like a bad word to me, as it was so painful to give up a role that was so close to my heart. I knew deep in my heart God had told me that it was time. In a similar way to how Abraham trusted in God, I needed to show that same trust with my position at church. However, giving up my role meant a part of my identity was gone, and I felt lost. I had to learn who I was without that part of me, which I admit I wasn't prepared to face at first.

From the day I stepped down, I experienced stages of grief. It was painful to be reminded every Sunday of that choice. Many causes of grief are out of our control, but this was my own decision. That is what made it more complicated and harder to explain to others. It still is. For me to start the healing process, I had to disengage completely from our church. My husband and I spent several Sundays going to a different church every week. I needed not to know what was going to happen to find a way to enjoy being in worship again. During this time, I was 99 percent sure that we would not be returning, but I chose to trust God to guide me in my grief process. Only after I felt God's peace to return were we able to go back. But even if we hadn't returned, I showed trust and faithfulness in worshipping through the grief. While the break was the beginning of my healing in this area, grief is something that can stay with you. "At first, grief is an ocean that pulls you under. With time, it becomes a river that you learn to swim in. But these waves...they never stop coming."[26]

When thinking about waves, it reminds me of a day of boogie boarding at Capitola Beach, just south of Santa Cruz, California. We had boogie boards to ride the waves. When you caught a good wave on the board, it took you all the way to shore. If you saw a bigger wave coming, it may have required a little paddling. You may not get the timing just right, but it was fun to try. If the wave was already crashing, it might pull you under the water and require you to swim out of it. The goal, of course, was to stay on top of the water.

While you want waves when boogie boarding, the waves provide a greater challenge when paddle boarding. My husband and I tried paddle boarding for the first time while at Lake Tahoe. The lake was calm to be able to first sit, then kneel, and then stand on the board. We took turns, and while Jeffrey was out paddling, getting the hang of it, a boat in the distance stirred the water, causing some ripples. If you're not steadied just right when the waves come, you can lose your balance and fall off the board. As Jeffrey was trying to reposition to be ready for the waves, he walked right off the board. Yep, we can walk right into moments of pain as well.

Unfortunately, a wave of grief can sneak up on you, and the emotions can overwhelm you, like being pulled under the water. When that wave hits, it may take using your coping skills like reaching out to a friend, distracting your mind with an activity, or letting those feelings work their way through tears. Or a combination of them all. As grief works through us, we can slowly get ourselves back on that board before the next wave hits.

While the word "worship" may still be altered by my experience of burnout, it also has helped me see worship in new ways. While it is important to worship in a church service, that is just the beginning. We can and should worship God in all areas of our lives. It can be in celebration, like Abraham, or in service, like Peter's mother-in-law, or even during a wave of grief. These examples show us that we can take all our emotions to God. Fortunately, when we are riding those waves, God will faithfully guide us to the shore every time.

REFLECTION QUESTIONS:

1. *When was a time that you struggled to worship through it?*

2. *What coping skills do you use during a wave of grief?*

Try a new way to worship through serving.

Song: "Hard Fought Hallelujah"

by Brandon Lake

(24.) Beauty for Ashes, "Worship isn't just sitting in a church pew," Facebook, February 9, 2025, https://www.facebook.com/hopeandhealingin JesusChrist/posts/pfbido27AKDmSC8v6dzwwW6FdbD9gNKVm93BJej U9WFGVriYCM9QR8VeqfRJnJopAtxqPYGl.

(25.) *NIV Quest Study Bible*, Grand Rapids, MI: Zondervan, 2001, p. 670.

(26.) Musings of a Poetic Soul, "At first, grief is an ocean," Facebook, May 25, 2025, https://www.facebook.com/MusingsOfAPoeticSoul/posts/ pfbido2crXJvYmWfKxGGjEkJCsnHtg12wsdPS565g6qxG1cx4Bat CGWPTotpvXee7gLZtE7l.

11

FELLOWSHIP BUILDING

"For where two or three gather in my name,
there am I with them."

(Matthew 18:20)

LIFE IS CHALLENGING WITH many twists and turns, even more so when we try to do it alone. It's crucial to build a community of believers, which requires fellowship with one another. The word "fellowship" is one of those church words we use when we think of activities within church walls. *Merriam-Webster's* definition is "a community of interest, activity, feeling, or experience."[27] The community of believers first began with the apostles and continues to build to the present day. God will help us build connections with new people who have had similar experiences, which builds our faith and community. While fellowship sounds like an easy ship to get on board, it can come with unexpected challenges.

Earlier, I spoke about how the apostles were first recruited and their struggles throughout Jesus's time. However, there is more to their stories, including casting out demons and healing others. Jesus first sent the Twelve to their fellow Jews. He then appointed an additional seventy-two to go ahead of him to prepare the way. In Jesus's instructions each time, he told them not to take any belongings or money with them. They were to find a worthy person and stay with them. If they felt welcomed in that home and town, they were to extend peace and healing. If not, they were to shake the dust off their sandals and give a warning of coming judgment.

Jesus's instruction to the Twelve also included a warning for them: "I am sending you out like sheep among wolves. Therefore be as shrewd as snakes and as innocent as doves. Be on your guard; you will be handed over to the local councils and be flogged in the synagogues" (Matthew 10:16–17). Wow! Sign me right up. I'm sure that's what you're thinking after that warning. No? Being one of those sent out meant more than glamorously casting out demons and healing the sick. They had to trust God and follow his instructions, even through sacrifices and pain. The lesson is to trust God in all moments, both highs and lows. While it may have been exciting in the beginning to follow Jesus, the honeymoon faded and the true tests of faithfulness began.

When Jesus sent out the apostles, he instructed them to go in pairs. These pairs were the beginning of the fellowship of believers. They were able to encourage one another and had a shared experience. Those moments strengthened not only their friendship, but also enabled them to share that fellowship with others. When I think about the activities I have participated in at my church, it's not about what we did, but how we experienced those moments together.

The illustrations Jesus uses for how we should act are fascinating as well. We are to be "sheep among wolves," which means to have an awareness that there will be people, wolves, wanting to attack you and your beliefs. A fear of being attacked is not very fellowship building, is it? The Jewish elite were already against Jesus's teachings because he challenged what the Jewish leaders were teaching. Despite the wolves we might face, we, the sheep, need our Shepherd in Jesus. He is our protector when we follow him, which means obeying his commands to spread the good news, no matter the risk.

The next analogy is to be as "shrewd as snakes." I find it interesting that while we have the image of a serpent tempting Eve in the Garden, this analogy puts the snake in a more positive light. To be shrewd means to discern or use wisdom. The snake is then paired with being as "innocent as doves," meaning to not sin so they can find no fault with you. Both animal analogies direct us to rely on the Holy Spirit to guide us in our steps. It can be tempting to want everyone to like you and to fit in. But we are called to show the love of Jesus, which sets us apart from the world.

While I don't have direct experience with any of those animals, I did have an interesting experience visiting a zoo in Australia. They had the softest koala, and you could pet it. This zoo also had the chance to feed kangaroos. Of course, I wanted to do that because when else would I get that chance? So, I grabbed an ice cream cone with the kangaroos' food and bent down to get a great photo of me feeding the kangaroos. What I didn't observe were the emus also in that area, and it's safe to say, they were hungry too. The next thing I knew, an emu was pecking at my hand for the food. What was supposed to be a calm and joyful moment turned into an attack by a more aggressive animal. Ok, attack may be a bit dramatic, but the emu did draw blood. The point is because I wasn't fully aware of my surroundings, I was caught off guard. The emus could be people on social media with an opposing view from us. They choose to nitpick at others and focus on arguing over showing grace. I was focused on the cute kangaroos and not on the emus who also wanted nourishment. We live in a world that has both kangaroos and emus. We need discernment from God on how to show God's love to everyone in person and online.

While following God's command to reach out to others can challenge our faith, it can also be an encouragement. It can be tempting to view fellowship as only fun-filled times with happy moments to share with others. However, my strongest relationships with fellow believers are with those who have been in the trenches with me. We have shown we will support one another in the good, bad, and ugly moments of our journey. Sharing about my mental health journey has helped me connect with others. My main point for those who are struggling is reminding them that God is always with them. In addition, for those who have someone in their life who struggles with mental health, I remind them that simple gestures like reaching out mean a lot to those struggling. While these are not new revelations, sharing about my struggles has created a safe space for others to be open about their struggles as well. It is tempting to feel like you are the only one struggling and to keep it all inside. I have found new connections with those who decide to share their struggles with me. As a result, those connections build up both people's faith through fellowship.

The apostles were also challenged to grow their fellowship after Jesus's death and resurrection. They were given the Holy Spirit on Pentecost and then were sent out again. But this time, it was to the ends of the earth. It can be challenging to fully understand what those experiences were like, but maybe not as different as we would like to think. Yes, a lot of people nowadays know about Jesus, but knowing is different than believing and following. Those attending a church service on Sundays is much lower than in previous generations, but Hebrews 10:25 warns us "not [to give] up meeting together, as some are in the habit of doing, but encouraging one another—and all the more as you see the Day approaching."

!REFLECTION QUESTIONS:

1. *What is a favorite moment of fellowship you have had?*

2. *How has God challenged you to step out of your comfort zone to extend fellowship to someone?*

Send a note or call someone you know
who is currently struggling.

Song: "Unashamed"

by Matthew West

(**27.**) Merriam Webster Online, s.v. "fellowship (n)," Accessed May 26, 2025, https://www.merriam-webster.com/dictionary/fellowship.

12

WHAT'S IN A TITHE?

*"God never gives you a dream that matches
your budget. He's not checking your bank account,
He's checking your faith."* [28]

STEWARDSHIP IS "THE CAREFUL and responsible management of something entrusted to one's care."[29] This includes how we manage our treasures (money and belongings), time, and talents. All throughout the Bible are examples of God showing us how giving is another way we show faithfulness. It is not just that we give, but that we give with the right attitude. Giving may require us to shift our mindset and challenge us to trust more than we think is possible.

The story of Cain and Abel is an example of stewardship. Both Cain and Abel brought offerings to God, but only Abel is shown favor from God. However, if you read closely, "Cain brought some of the fruits of the soil" while Abel brought "fat portions from some of the firstborn of his flock" (Genesis 4:3–4). Abel made sure to offer the best part of the first animals. It isn't clear how Cain chose his offering. Was it the best fruit off the trees? Was the offering first in his mind or an afterthought? "By faith Abel brought God a better offering than Cain did" (Hebrews 11:4). So it isn't just what we give, but our attitude—we want to give, not we have to give. God wants us to give our best, not our leftovers, because he has given so much to us.

There are many examples in the Old Testament about how we are to offer our first fruits. Abraham gave a tenth of everything to Melchizedek. This is the first mention of tithing, which means a tenth. "It was a sign of his gratitude to God and a sign that he had submitted to Melchizedek and would not compete with him."[30] This highlights another characteristic of stewardship—submission. We show our gratitude to God by showing him he is the one in control. He brought everything into existence, including us. The fact that he only asks us for ten percent of what we have is humbling in itself. God does ask us for all our heart and reliance on him. Giving our first fruits is how we show we have put God first in our lives.

Tithing was included in the Law to provide support for the Levites in their service to God in the tabernacle and then the temple. They had no income of their own, so they relied on others for support. The book of Malachi included a section on tithing. "'Bring the whole tithe into the storehouse, that there may be food in my house. Test me in this,' says the LORD Almighty, 'and see if I will not throw open the floodgates of heaven and pour out so much blessing that there will not be room enough to store it'" (Malachi 3:10). This was an interesting twist on testing God's Word. The people first needed to show trust by giving their entire tithe and trusting God to provide for them. I understand if people hesitated on this challenge as it is quite hard to fully let go. But, like with Abram, it is more about our posture of submission over the specific sacrifice.

What I found intriguing was tithing was part of the last message Jewish people heard from God before four hundred years of silence. The final part of the message was that God would be there, trust him, and do what they knew to do. When someone is no longer in your life, whether through death, a break up, or drifting apart, you think back to the last conversations you had. Those can be comforting, painful, or both. The Jewish people had gone through many forms of breakups, starting with the split into two kingdoms. Then the Kingdoms of Israel and Judah were conquered by the Assyrians, and then the Babylonians. The Jewish people were taken into exile multiple times, and some fled to Egypt. When the people were able to return, it may have been multiple generations after they had been exiled. Their connection to their past had been altered by the seasons they were away from the Promised Land. What a test of faithfulness. Would they continue to seek God, or let these times of separation further distance themselves from him? Would they remember what God had told them to do, including stewardship?

These questions bring up another. How did the time of silence prepare the people for the coming Messiah? Since many people were far from the temple, they created places of worship in their own areas. This helped show the people they could seek God where they were, not just in the temple. But it also influenced stewardship; they shifted their tithes to the poor and local Jewish leaders. Unfortunately, the leaders in the temple also shifted to more corrupt collections in the area where the Gentiles would worship, as the story of Jesus overturning the tables of the money changers showed (Matthew 21). Jesus showed us that some shifts in our lives are necessary to reset our priorities, to seek God first and not our comforts and desires.

Jesus further shifted people's thinking about stewardship with the story of the widow's offering. Jesus was watching as people put in their money at the temple treasury boxes. As the rich people put in many coins, which would have been noisy, they caught the attention and admiration from others. Then a widow stepped up and put in her last two coins. Jesus brought attention to this, saying, "Truly I tell you, this poor widow has put more into the treasury than all the others. They all gave out of their wealth; but she, out of her poverty, put in everything—all she had to live on" (Mark 12:43–44). This woman's example of trusting God over worldly possessions is quite shocking. I am striving to have that high level of faithfulness and trust in God. Remembering what Jesus did on the cross by sacrificing himself, even to death, reminds me of his faithfulness, which helps me trust him more. Jesus raised the bar of stewardship by showing it will include sacrificing our own needs and comforts.

When I was thinking of new stories for this book, a funny story about trying to meet high expectations came to mind. When my husband and I went to Germany in 2010, the friends we were visiting thought it would be fun to take us to the grocery store. They needed to get some supplies. The store seemed similar to our stores here until we got to the checkout line. They explained that the clerk only rings up the items; the bagging was up to us. We then learned that the clerk was timed on how quickly she could scan all the items. My husband was up to the challenge to grab the items while our friend put the items on the conveyor belt. He was okay at first, but then the speed picked up, and the items just kept filling the counter. Our friend also had to strategize how she put the items on the conveyor belt, so the cans didn't smash the bread. Thankfully, the clerk was aware this was my husband's first time and slowed down just a little. Jeffrey made it through loading all the items in the cart. While it was a funny story, it reminded me that while he had the right attitude and gave his full energy, he couldn't meet that high bar of expectation. Unlike the clerk who didn't help my husband, Jesus made it possible for us to reach up to God by shifting all our sins onto himself and paying the cost.

In today's world, it may feel like we are always being asked to give more, whether it's our money, time, or talent. But, if we are wise, we will understand our contributions are just a drop in the bucket. Praise God for his 100 percent commitment to us.

REFLECTION QUESTIONS:

1. *Put yourself in the widow's shoes. How do you think she had the faith to put all her money in?*

2. *How does having the right attitude towards giving help build your faith?*

ACT OF FAITHFULNESS

*Find a local organization you can give an offering to
of your time, talents, and/or treasures.*

Song: "Greater"

by MercyMe

(28.) Faith Remedy, "God never gives you a dream," Facebook, December 6, 2025, https://www.facebook.com/faithremedy/posts/pfbidoPzB WsWAmn2f66DiaAuWLTGZtXo3BnBUat3EK94YDq7MfmuKdXe8iin Ukw9vtEW6Zl.

(29.) Merriam Webster Online, s.v. "stewardship (n)," Accessed May 20, 2025, https://www.merriam-webster.com/dictionary/stewardship.

(30.) *NIV Quest Study Bible*, Grand Rapids, MI: Zondervan, 2001, p. 21.

13

FRIENDSHIP BONDS

*"Many people will walk in and out of your life,
but only true friends will leave footprints
in your heart."* [31]

FRIENDSHIPS ARE IMPORTANT ON our journey, both with God and other people. These relationships help to build our confidence and pursue God's calling in our lives. While we are not to rely solely on the support from others, we are stronger together. Friends can help us and encourage us to keep going. Sometimes, the faith of others carries us when we feel we can't hold onto it ourselves.

When I was asked who in the Bible I can relate most to, my answer was Elijah. Not because he is well-known, but because I can relate to his journey the most. Elijah arrived on the scene telling King Ahab there would be no rain until Elijah gave the word. He then fled to Cherith, a creek, and spent an unspecified amount of time there. He was alone for likely several months, being fed by God through ravens. Elijah built his friendship with God by obeying and trusting him to provide sustenance. After some time, Elijah was tasked with finding a widow in Zarephath, a Gentile city full of Baal worshippers, but that was all he was told. He found the woman, though we don't learn her name, and asked her for a drink and some bread. Her response was she had only enough for one more meal for her son and herself, and then they would die. But she put her trust in Elijah's God and obeyed Elijah's request. Because of her faithfulness, the flour and oil never ran dry the entire time Elijah stayed with her, which was several more months. Sometimes, a relationship can develop with people whom we wouldn't have predicted.

After three years, it was time for Elijah to confront King Ahab and the Baal prophets. They met on Mt. Carmel. Elijah had learned there were many other prophets of God who had been in hiding, but when he stood on Mt. Carmel, no one else stepped forward to declare they would follow God. That silence must have been heartbreaking, and yet Elijah put his trust in God. Both the Baal prophets and Elijah built an altar with a sacrificial bull, and whoever's god answered by fire was *the* God. The Baal prophets tried for hours with no response. When it was Elijah's turn, he upped the ante and used water to douse the altar and surrounding area, which made a fire impossible. But it was not impossible for God. We may think our situation is beyond help, that we're drowning, but that's when God shows us his mercy, if we're willing to seek him.

After the spectacular defeat of all the Baal prophets, Elijah was given a new death threat from King Ahab's wife, Jezebel. Elijah ran and was at his lowest point because he had had enough. He was done with life. But God sent an angel to comfort him. He was then sent to a cave. One of my favorite lines in the Bible is when God asked him, "What are you doing here, Elijah?" (1 Kings 19:9). God then instructed Elijah to go out and the LORD would pass by, but he didn't say how. It was not in the wind, in an earthquake, or in a fire, but in a whisper. Doesn't that sound about right? We must get still to fully hear God, away from all the noise of the world and in our heads. Hearing from God will probably not be in grandiose ways for us either.

Then God asks Elijah that same question: "What are you doing here?" It can be tempting to think once you finish serving in one area, you can't move onto something else. Elijah may have thought God wouldn't use him again after his lowest moment, but God showed him it wasn't the end of his story. After God asked him that question, he then sent Elijah to find Elisha. This was someone he could befriend and be a mentor to. God knew Elijah could use his experiences to guide others. It must have been a good feeling for Elijah to finally be able to freely connect with a fellow prophet. Like Elijah, we may have times of preparation and showing faithfulness before God moves us onto guiding others.

I relate to Elijah in many ways. When God first called Elijah to stand up to King Ahab, he then was sent to the creek. This can be seen as a wilderness time, where he was challenged in his faithfulness to God. When I felt called to pursue my dream of writing, my struggles with my mental health spiked. As I wrote about challenging times in my life, I saw where God was with me. As my first book came together, I sought help from people I didn't know and yet trusted. It wasn't as extreme as being sent to a foreign land, but navigating the land of publishing and marketing felt nerve-wracking and put me out of my comfort zone. When my first book came out in 2021, I can understand the stand Elijah took on Mt. Carmel. No, I didn't go kill Baal prophets, but it was me standing up as a believer in God for all to see.

While others were there to support me, it was just me on this journey. And yes, that was terrifying and sent me on a downward spiral. I understand Elijah running away and asking for death to come. While I had just written about how God was with me in past events, I couldn't stop myself from believing the lie that I was alone. But even though, like Elijah, I wanted to die, God comforted me and helped me through my darkest moments. I like the part in the story when after

Elijah doused the altar, God came and burned up the entire sacrifice. I like it because when I was really struggling with my mental health, my pastor told me, "Sometimes you have to burn it all down," which meant sometimes we need a full reset in our lives. It doesn't mean all was fixed and healed after I spent a few days in a psychiatric unit. It meant that it was the beginning of the next phase of growing my trust and friendship with God.

Because of my lowest moments, I doubted God would ever use me again. Yet, after some time passed, I felt the call to write again. Like God's question of "What are you doing here?" I felt the nudging to get up and pursue my writing dream further. My story can show others they are not alone either. I know my experiences have shown me the love and friendship of God, which I can now share with others. As we heal from our past hurts or grief, we may not see progress while we are in the situation, but when we take a step back, it becomes clearer. "Maybe you don't see your progress because you are always raising the bar. Take a moment to look back— you have already achieved things you once thought were impossible."[32] If God has called you to do something, he will give you the faith to complete it.

While friendship with God comes first, the ways others show up when you need support is priceless. I recently came across a journal entry from a retreat when I was fifteen. It described a night when I felt God spoke to me about not committing suicide. I was kneeling in a chapel with new friends, holding hands as we cried. We had just watched a video about Jesus's last hours, which described the pain and suffering he went through. My tears were a release of emotion as I realized the pain and suffering people go through in their last hours. I was grieving both Jesus's death and the death of a beloved teacher that had passed the year before.

After we left the church, I went to the hallway outside my room. One of our adult leaders, Chad, came over, sat down, put his arm around me, and let me cry. I don't remember if anything was said in those moments, but I felt the love and friendship of having someone be there with me. We may think we need to know exactly what to say to someone who is struggling, but it meant more to me that he was willing to just be present with me. I am thankful I found this entry as I didn't remember what happened after sitting in the hallway. I went back to the church, which is probably when I had my moment with God, and then I went to tell the adult leaders goodnight. Each one got up and gave me a hug, which also helped me feel like I wasn't alone. I believe it was nights like that which turned me into a hugger because I know the importance of that connection. That night, God showed me how I am not alone and how he and other people care about me. Remembering that love has helped me want to live.

While we may not stay connected with certain people throughout our lives, we can take the moments we shared with them with us. God is with us through it all and will guide us to the people we need.

REFLECTION QUESTIONS:

1. *Who in the Bible do you relate to most?*

2. *How can showing support be a way to build someone's faith?*

Think of a friend who had an impact on your faith.
Reach out to them and thank them.

Song: "Trust in God"

by Elevation Worship

(31.) Eleanor Roosevelt. "People come in and out of your life," AZ Quotes, Accessed September 24, 2025, https://www.azquotes.com/quote/354785?ref=people-in-your-life.

(32.) @drcarolineleaf, "Maybe you don't see your progress," Instagram, November 27, 2024, https://www.instagram.com/p/DC4XrK5JWo2/?utm_source=ig_web_copy_link&igsh=MzRlODBiNWFlZA==.

14

I DIDN'T SIGN UP FOR HARDSHIP

*"A ship in the harbor is safe, but that's not
what ships are built for."* [33]

WHEN WE HEAR THE word "hardship," it can bring up unpleasant memories and emotions. We want to avoid suffering or hardship of any kind because it's uncomfortable and plain no fun to go through. As believers, we are called to not stay in the safety of the harbor, but with that comes risk. Leaving the harbor can challenge where you place your priorities and your faithfulness. Hardships can push you to what you may think is your limit, but God may take you further.

When I thought about who dealt with a lot of hardships in the Bible, I went to Paul. He was first named Saul and persecuted new believers of the Way (new Christians). As Saul was on his way to Damascus to throw more believers into prison, God stepped in. "Suddenly a light from heaven flashed around him. He fell to the ground and heard a voice say to him, 'Saul, Saul, why do you persecute me?' [Saul asked,] 'Who are you, Lord?'" (Acts 9:3–5). Jesus replied it was him and then gave instructions for what to do next. Saul then realized he was blind and was escorted to a home in Damascus. Sometimes we need to go through a hardship to be able to see truth more clearly.

The next part of the story required the faithfulness of another believer. God called a man named Ananias to go to Saul and heal his blindness. Ananias showed his faithfulness to God as he knew about Saul and his persecution and went anyways. God told him, "I will show him how much he [Saul] must suffer for my name" (Acts 9:16). After Saul was healed, he was baptized and started regaining his strength. God will use anyone who is willing to turn from their own ways to be a disciple. Both Saul and Ananias had to surrender their own prejudgments to be faithful to God.

Paul confirmed how he suffered for God through the many ways he had been tortured and exposed to death. "Five times I received from the Jews the forty lashes minus one. Three times I was beaten with rods, once I was pelted with stones, three times I was shipwrecked, I spent a night and a day in the open sea, I have been constantly on the move" (2 Corinthians 11:24–26). That was just part of what he went through. Paul doesn't give a number for how many times he was in prison, made daring escapes out of cities, and went without the basics. I can't imagine any of those experiences, and to have gone through them multiple times had to have worn him down. If it had been me, I would be questioning if I could continue.

While Paul mentioned being shipwrecked three times, we only have one of the stories. Paul was arrested and, because he didn't believe he would have a fair trial in the Jewish courts, he appealed to Caesar, which meant he had to be sent to Rome. The first part of the trip was fine, but then a storm hit. It slowly built from a gentle wind to hurricane strength. The men on the ship tried what they knew to do, but after several days of this storm, hope was waning. Paul assured them God would keep them safe and to eat to keep up their strength. The ship finally ran aground in shallow water. Paul continued his ministry on the island until he finally made it to Rome. While it is not clear from the Bible how or when Paul died, the book of Acts concludes with, "He proclaimed the kingdom of God and taught about the Lord Jesus Christ—with all boldness and without hindrance" (Acts 28:31). That is quite a testimony of showing faithfulness through all types of hardship.

While we may not have personally experienced anything like Paul, we all have had moments that pushed us to decide to face a challenge or not. That decision could be changing careers, moving to another city, standing up for what you believe, or even having the strength to keep going. As I shared in the previous chapter of being told to "burn it all down," it required strength to make the decision to get help. I drove myself to the hospital, walked in, and said I was having suicidal ideation. That was the most terrifying thing I have ever done. It meant I had to reveal my darkest thoughts, ones that came with so much guilt and shame. But it also meant I was surrendering control of my fate. As the nurse walked me to a room, I remember her telling the security guard that I was one of his, which meant he needed to keep an eye on me. Hours passed in the ER with basic tests, a psychological evaluation, and looking for a placement in a psychiatric unit. Slowly, the reality of it all hit. As the hours dragged on, I started getting more anxious and agitated and wanted to just go home. Once we knew where I would be going, my husband left. I am thankful he did because I believe I would have kept bugging him to go home. Since the thoughts of wanting to die were only subdued in the hospital, I imagine they would have come back quickly if I had gone home. For this reason, I believe his leaving me there in the hospital kept me alive.

When it was finally time to be taken to the facility, I was escorted out by security. I don't remember what the guard said as I got into the car, but it was encouraging and something he didn't have to do. By the time I finished my intake at the facility, I had been stripped of almost all my belongings. While I have never been arrested or spent time in a prison, those few days in a facility gave me glimpses. The first full day I was there was the day for visitors. I saw it on the schedule, and even though I knew in my head my husband loved me, I didn't believe he would come. My fear of abandonment was trying to take over my feelings of self-worth. To my surprise, he did come and asked me why I didn't call him the night before or that morning. I remember thinking I didn't want to wake him, like he would have slept just fine and not be worried about me. That visit gave me hope I wasn't as alone as I was feeling. I can better understand how lonely the days in prison are without the comforts and people from home.

The questions about my suicidal plans continued every day. I thought I would get help from a therapist, and when I asked, I was told, "You need to work out your emotional distress on your own." Telling someone who is on suicidal watch that they need to work out their own issues didn't make sense. It was the reason why I sought help. When the one psychiatrist questioned me about my plans, he made a point of telling me how horrible it would have been if I had followed through. Um, yeah, I know. I felt God wouldn't want to forgive me for the plans I had, which came with a lot of guilt and shame. Like Saul, God erased my past, but I had to accept his forgiveness.

While I was disappointed in the lack of therapy from the facility, I was safe from myself. The staff I remember were the ones, like the security guard, who saw me as a person, not a number. The other patients there helped pass the time. While we were all there on the suicidal watch unit, a few were open about their failed suicide attempts. Even with the seriousness of the unit we were on, getting checked on every fifteen minutes, we were able to find humor. To be able to laugh amidst all the pain we were suffering with showed us we could still have joy. Healing, even if it was just the next breath, had begun.

What this time of hardship taught me was while you may feel like you are in a prison, you can still have hope. Paul showed us that while in prison, he was singing, sharing about God, and encouraging others on their journey. I learned there are some moments that may be terrifying to do alone, but God will walk with us faithfully. We may not feel like we are being faithful and will likely have moments when we aren't. But thankfully, God shows us that we are worthy of his love and puts people in our lives to help show us we are. We also can see we are stronger than we think we are. I made the choice to live and, even more so, to live for Christ. While it takes time to heal from each hardship we go through, if we endure, we can then help others in theirs. While hardships are hard, we can get through anything with God's help.

REFLECTION QUESTIONS:

1. *How did your faith grow during a hardship?*

2. *How can your experience of hardship be used to help others?*

Send a word of encouragement to someone who is going through a hardship.

Song: "Oceans (Where Feet May Fail)"
by Hillsong United

(33.) John A Shedd, "A ship in the harbour," Goodreads, accessed September 24, 2025, https://www.goodreads.com/author/quotes/5171938.John_A_Shedd.

15

BLIND DISCIPLESHIP

"When God gives you a vision, when he lays something on your heart…see it through. Sometimes following Him looks really, really crazy to everyone else, but when you step out on faith, He will never fail to meet you there." [34]

THE JOURNEY OF DISCIPLESHIP can challenge us to take blind steps of faith. "Discipleship, at its core, is about becoming a devoted follower of Jesus Christ. It involves a personal journey of growth where one learns the teachings of Christ, embraces His lifestyle, and commits to living out those principles daily."[35]

It is also where God can reveal himself, if we are looking. Paul referenced Isaiah 64:4 when he wrote, "'What no eye has seen, what no ear has heard, and what no human mind has conceived'—the things God has prepared for those who love him—these are the things God has revealed to us by his Spirit" (1 Corinthians 2:9–10). The stories that make this Scripture come alive include blind men seeing, Zaccheus, Thomas, and the walk to Emmaus.

There are a few different accounts of Jesus healing the blind in the Bible. In Luke 18:38, a blind man was crying out to Jesus, saying, "Jesus, Son of David, have mercy on me!" He recognized Jesus as the Messiah, even if he couldn't physically see. I have heard our other senses are heightened when we are deficient in one. In this case, this heightened sense the blind man had was his faith. Jesus told him it was because of his faith that he was healed, and immediately, this man followed Jesus. What a testimony of faith this man could now give as a disciple!

Another man could physically see, but strived to see better. Yes, I am talking about Zaccheus, who climbed a tree to be able to see Jesus as he walked by. Jesus noticed Zaccheus and then told him that he was heading to Zaccheus's home. The people there couldn't believe Jesus would spend time with a sinful tax collector. Despite his wealth, Zaccheus didn't try to buy his way into time with Jesus. I believe Jesus saw his heart and that Zaccheus repented. Zaccheus said, "Look, Lord! Here and now I give half of my possessions to the poor, and if I have cheated anybody out of anything, I will pay back four times the amount" (Luke 19:8). Zaccheus was looked down upon in his community for his role. He was now able to see how his greed was sinful, which made him willing to go above and beyond to make amends. He could also better see how helping others is a big part of discipleship.

While these two men had short encounters with Jesus, Thomas was one of his disciples. He had witnessed many of these miracles and was able to hear Jesus's predictions about what was to happen, namely his death and resurrection. However, even seeing and hearing all these things, Thomas still wanted to see proof for himself. He had been absent the first time Jesus appeared to the disciples after his resurrection. While the other disciples told him what happened, Thomas said, "Unless I see the nail marks in his hands and put my finger where the nails were, and put my hand into his side, I will not believe" (John 20:25). He had to wait a few days for this opportunity, and when Jesus came, Jesus didn't condemn him for his lack of faith. Jesus gave Thomas the chance to touch him, to stop doubting and believe. Though the Bible doesn't say whether Thomas touched Jesus, it does say that Thomas acknowledged Jesus as Lord. While we also would like to see Jesus, his next statement applies to us: "Because you have seen me, you have believed; blessed are those who have not seen and yet have believed" (John 20:29). Believing in something that we have not seen or heard in the natural sense is the definition of faith. However, God gives us signs all around us, if we are willing to look.

The walk to Emmaus is an example of people not seeing what was right in front of them. Two men were returning home to Emmaus from Jerusalem. Jesus joined them, but they are kept from recognizing him. Jesus listened as the men talked about how they had hoped Jesus would have redeemed Israel, but was put to death instead. They knew Jesus's body was no longer in the tomb, but didn't understand that he was resurrected. Jesus then explained all the Scripture concerning himself. However, it wasn't until Jesus broke bread with them that their eyes were opened. "They asked each other, 'Were not our hearts burning within us while he talked with us on the road and opened the Scriptures to us?'" (Luke 24:32). While these men didn't recognize Jesus immediately, it shows us that sometimes God withholds showing us something until his timing. I have had moments in my life when I have wondered, why didn't I see something before? But it may mean we needed to have a certain experience to be able see it in a new light.

I have learned many of these lessons about sight through my dogs. Though I could use examples from my previous books, luckily, I have more stories. They revolve around our dog Shadow as she grew older. One thing we cannot see well, or admit, is how our bodies change as we get older. Shadow used to be able to run down the stairs and out to chase the squirrels or bark at the mailman. But the times of running became less frequent and for shorter distances. While she persevered to an amazing age of almost fifteen, we noticed her declining for a couple years.

We have a split-level house, and the dogs generally sleep upstairs in our bedroom. Sometimes Shadow was able to navigate our stairs smoothly, but other times she tumbled down the stairs, which was sad to watch. I can best describe it as her trying to hop down the stairs, but her back legs just couldn't handle it. We had to help her get back up many times at the bottom of those stairs. Shadow also tended to back up as she sat down, and there were several times when she backed up too much and started to slip down the stairs. If we could react quickly, we could stop the sliding and help her back up to our main floor. She would look so helpless, like one of those roly-polies that are on their backs with their feet in the air. Or Shadow would try to get all the way up the stairs with us right behind to help her. All these moments remind me how things change. Sometimes we may need to modify how we approach the situation, such as a physical change, where we invest our energy, or how we serve God. It can be hard to accept these changes, but we need to seek insight on when it may be time to let go.

While Shadow was not completely blind, we could see her vision had changed. She would stand at the top of the stairs, and sometimes would step down one, then stop. Her hesitation showed a lack of confidence in her next step. We may also lack confidence in our next step of faith. Like we were able to help Shadow navigate each struggle with the steps, God is also right there to hold our hand in all our struggles. While we cannot see God like Thomas got the chance to see Jesus, we can see God through others as they help us.

I mentioned earlier about Shadow chasing squirrels. As Shadow's speed slowed, and our other dog Pasha's eyesight waned, one squirrel became bolder in where he would walk in our yard. This included drinking out of the dogs' water bucket or letting himself inside to grab a bite of food if our door was open. Of course, we would shoo him away, but he knew he was safe. A few months after we put Pasha down, we added a new dog to our family, Hazley. Well, Shadow and Hazley were both black labs. In Hazley's first few days, she made her presence known. The squirrel was getting closer to the house when Hazley saw him and took off after him. I'm sure the squirrel had thought it was just slow Shadow, but Hazley almost caught him on her first try. The squirrel learned that not everything was as it appeared. Those types of moments can be jarring at first, like the men walking to Emmaus. But once they saw the truth, their lives would never be the same.

The journey of a disciple requires us to trust which steps to take, even though we cannot see the full path. However, if we remain open to being faithful in each step, we will have peace in knowing we are not alone. We have God and others we will meet on the way who will show us what we need to see.

REFLECTION QUESTIONS:

1. *When did you experience something you knew was a sign from God?*

2. *What was one change in your life that required you to trust without seeing?*

Open your Bible to one of the parables Jesus taught.
As you read it, let God show you something new in the story.

Song: "No Fear"

by Jon Reddick

(34.) Annie Stewart Lambert. "When God gives you a vision," Facebook, July 18, 2025, https://www.facebook.com/anniestewart82/posts/pfbido RWgEcd6iPwbiFEN1jAn9M7HyMPc1v4vf4oJSWnmXKJULbUmZPip FxUwVR6WQ5nQYl.

(35.) "How Mission Trips Encourage Discipleship and Evangelism," I mpact Ministries & Retreat Center, Accessed June 27, 2025, https:// www.impactmb.org/single-post/how-mission-trips-encourage-discipleship-and-evangelism.

16

WHO DO YOU BREAK BREAD WITH?

"Faith in God is not an emotional response,
but a deliberate decision to trust and rely on God
even when the road ahead seems uncertain." [36]

WHO DO YOU THINK of when you hear the word "companion"? Most likely, the answer is a spouse or partner. The word companion is derived from Latin *com,* meaning "with," and *panis,* meaning "food or bread."[37] Put together, companionship extrapolates to who you break bread or eat meals with. It makes sense that we associate companionship with a romantic relationship, as we share a lot of meals together. Choosing a romantic partner should be made with God's guidance as this kind of relationship takes commitment and trust for the long haul. All people we choose to walk with, including our romantic partner, challenge us to do what Jesus would do: forgive, show grace and mercy, and love them as they are.

While there are many examples in the Bible of couples, I felt led to the story of Hosea and Gomer. It may sound like an odd choice at first glance. If you're unfamiliar with their story, it began with the Lord speaking to Hosea, saying, "Go, marry a promiscuous woman and have children with her, for like an adulterous wife this land is guilty of unfaithfulness to the LORD" (Hosea 1:2). Whoa. That's a lot to unpack. Hosea was instructed to risk his reputation, amongst other things, by who he chose as his wife. But Hosea was faithful and did what God instructed him to do.

Hosea and Gomer then had three children. The meaning of the names God instructed them were just as shocking as being told to marry an adulterer. Jezreel means "God scatters," Lo-Ruhamah means "not loved," and Lo-Ammi means "not my people" (Hosea 1). Whoa again. The people in that time took the meaning of names as messages, so what was God's message to them? The entire book of Hosea was about God's relationship with his people and how they had been unfaithful. Jezreel referred to a warning of upcoming judgment or being scattered. The other children's names, not loved and not my people, showed how the people's unfaithfulness had led to separation from God. The lesson is to remember to seek God, and even when we voice our pain to God, he will not leave us.

One twist in the Hosea story was when Gomer left him and was with another man, committing adultery. One may think God would have let Hosea go in another direction, but God prompted Hosea to go get his wife back. Thankfully, in Hosea's marriage and children, God showed his willingness to forgive all forms of unfaithfulness. There may be times in our lives when we are tempted to run away from a relationship or situation. Whether we run away or not, God directs us to forgive, as we have been forgiven. Once we let go of the past, we can seek reconciliation, but only if the peace of God guides us to reunification.

But why would God tell Hosea to marry Gomer in the first place? "God called other prophets to integrate their lives into the messages they proclaimed, yet no prophet endured what Hosea endured."[38] Yes, Job could be the prophet who endured more suffering. But as God allowed Job's suffering, God directed Hosea to endure what he did. We often choose our partner based on compatibility, common interests, and companionship, but sometimes we want someone who also challenges us. Being challenged is not limited to a romantic partner. We can learn and grow in all relationships. It could be a friend who holds you accountable, who also supports you in tough moments. These relationships may feel like they were random in how they began, but I believe God has his hand in who crosses our paths and when. I have had many people come into my life at what felt like just the right time to show me how I am not alone in an area, including in my mental health struggles. Sometimes it is fellow writers, a new friendship, or reconnecting with someone I knew years ago. Relationships can put our faith to the test. But like the story of Hosea showed, our experiences will give us more authenticity when we share about God to others.

The image of a marriage is used to describe Christ's relationship with the Church as his bride. One description Paul used to describe this relationship was, "I am jealous for you with a godly jealousy. I promised you to one husband, to Christ, so that I might present you as a pure virgin to him" (2 Corinthians 11:2). Christ, as the bridegroom, is head of the church, and we, as believers, are to commit our lives to be unified with Christ. In contrast to Gomer's past, we are to be presented as pure when this union occurs. But how can we be seen as pure? That is what Christ's crucifixion was for: to cover all our sins so we will be seen as blameless. The forgiveness of sins, while it is offered, must also be received by each believer. The culmination of this union is described in the book of Revelation, when the wedding feast will occur. This union is eternal and where God will be with his people. That is a companionship we all can have. Other relationships have their missteps and shortcomings, but our relationship with God will be perfect in heaven.

While Hosea's story had a lot of strife in it, the story I want to share is much lighter. My husband, Jeffrey, has been there for me in some of my darkest moments. He also has been my support in my writing journey, helping me with many of my book events. He doesn't really like to read, so it is quite amusing how much time he has spent in bookstores just for me. But this story is about something I did for him. I was a willing participant, but you'll see where it pushed me out of my comfort zone.

Since we live in Colorado, we decided we would go skiing for a day. I had been a whopping two previous times, so my skills and confidence were limited. The first time I ever went skiing, I struggled with even getting on the ski lift. When it was our turn to get up to the designated line, I crossed my skis and fell over. I was aware enough to duck as the chair lift was swinging around, avoiding it smacking right into me. I was helped up and onto the chair lift. Dismounting the ski lift feels like an Olympic skill that I never got down. I told my husband my skill level, or lack of it, but he was willing to try to help me anyways. He held my arm as we dismounted, so we clumsily made it off together.

We spent our time going down the beginner trails, which was going alright. Then we watched some people go a different way off the ski lift, so we decided to follow them. We realized quickly we were on an intermediate trail. I was not thrilled as it was terrifying watching the other skiers zoom past quickly. But we were committed to the trail. There was no turning back. Jeffrey was there to encourage me. He stayed with me as I skied a short stretch before the fear of going too fast took over and I would stop. I would let the other skiers go by as I got up the courage to keep going. It was something I didn't feel prepared for at all, but my companion never left me. Although I was scared to step out of my comfort zone, I now can say I have skied an intermediate trail. Our faith journey can feel like that intermediate trail. We can watch other people seem to sail through their journey while we are struggling to get to the next step. Thankfully, we can lean on our fellow companions and, most importantly, God to help us.

While you may not understand why God tells you to do something, know God has only the purest of intentions. It may mean seeking new relationships, severing others, or returning to a painful situation. It may also mean forgiving when you don't feel it has been earned. But, as God has forgiven our sins, in turn, we are called to show forgiveness. If, like me, you struggle to forgive at times, know God will be your companion to guide you through it. Then, like Hosea, we can spread the good news with our own unique story.

REFLECTION QUESTIONS:

1. *What relationship started in your life when you needed it?*

2. *How did a companion help you build your faith?*

Ask God to show you anyone you need to forgive
and give you the grace to do it.

Song: "Faithfully"

by TobyMac

(36.) My Bible and God, "Faith in God is not an emotional response," Facebook, September 14, 2024, https://www.facebook.com/MyBibleAndGod/posts/ pfbidoeAu4x6jwBiuSN4jcQqRVHt6jec3LZhMEzBAmioUFewN F2bDgw1yBjKUkL1HGppv6l.

(37.) Merriam Webster Online, "Breaking Bread with 'Companion,'" Accessed July 6, 2025, https://www.merriam-webster.com/wordplay/ history-of-word-companion.

(38.) *NIV Quest Study Bible*, Grand Rapids, MI: Zondervan, 2001, p. 1318.

17

GOING INTO BATTLE

*"A Christian never falls asleep in the fire or in the water,
but grows drowsy in the sunshine."* [39]

WHILE WE WOULD LOVE to view our faith as sailing along on a day trip, the truth is it is better described as a being on a battleship, day in and day out. Life can feel like we are being hit from all angles. If we're not aware of how to defend ourselves from these attacks, it can overwhelm us, like a wave in a storm. Thankfully, we have tools to use, like prayer, to help us every day to not only defend the attacks, but to go on the offensive. We also need to use discernment for which battles God is calling us to fight.

When you go into battle, you want to go in prepared, including wearing armor. Paul described the armor of God in the book of Ephesians. This included the belt of truth, the breastplate of righteousness, the shoes of peace, the shield of faith, the helmet of salvation, and the sword of the Spirit. Since this book is about faithfulness, we'll focus on the shield of faith. "In addition to all this, take up the shield of faith, with which you can extinguish all the flaming arrows of the evil one" (Ephesians 6:16). In a study about the armor of God, Priscilla Shirer explained what this shield would look like:

"He was referencing a larger shield that was typically two feet wide and four feet long, shaped almost like a door, consisting of planks of wood fused together. The wood was covered by canvas. Then by leather. Then iron was built into the center as a hub and also onto the extreme edges of the shield from top to bottom."[40]

This description helps us understand all the layers of protection a soldier had. Later in her study, she described how the soldiers would interlock the shields together and pour water on them so the flaming arrows would be doused. Both of those details are important as we are stronger when we are with others and when we use all our resources to deflect the enemy. The biggest tool we have is prayer, both on our own and in groups.

Jesus was seen praying many times. He prayed for three things in the seventeenth chapter of the Gospel of John. First, he prayed for God to be glorified in his actions. He knew what suffering was to come and knew he needed strength to fulfill God's will. Second, he prayed for his disciples. He knew they had a very challenging road ahead to spread the good news after Jesus's death. He knew he was returning to his Father, but was leaving behind his followers. He prayed for their protection: "My prayer is not that you take them out of the world but that you protect them from the evil one" (John 17:15). Jesus was helping them take up their shields.

Third, Jesus prayed for future believers. He prayed for all of us to believe God had sent him and God loves us. In both prayers, for the disciples and future believers, Jesus prayed, "That all of them may be one, Father, just as you are in me and I am in you" (John 17:21). Jesus wanted all of us to have the same relationship that he had with his Father. Not Jesus above us, but as equals. While we have many Chrisian denominations, we are all unified in our belief in Christ. That is a powerful thought. No matter if our style of worshipping God varies, we can all show one another the love of Christ.

The love of Christ can be as hot as the flaming arrows coming our way. The battle we are in isn't just us cowering in a corner and ducking to avoid getting hit. Sometimes we need to be prepared to fight back with faith. David as a shepherd boy was bold enough to face Goliath with just a slingshot, five stones, and a whole lot of faith. If David was unsuccessful, the Israelites would become servants to the Philistines. David's faith in God convinced King Saul to let

David take the risk. David knocked Goliath down on his first shot and then took Goliath's sword to finish the job. I like that David used the enemy's weapon against him. They had tried to put Saul's armor on him, but because David wasn't used to wearing it, he felt hindered by the equipment. The lesson is we need to use discernment on what we use and how we approach our battles.

David also showed boldness and openness when he wrote the Psalms. What I can appreciate is he took everything he felt to God. The good, the bad, and even the ugly. That's authentic prayer. We may think we'll never be faced with something like David to be able to show our boldness in faith. However, we may sell ourselves short if our desire to stay in our comfort zone outweighs our faith. Or as in one of the churches in the book in Revelation was told, "I know your deeds, that you are neither cold nor hot. I wish you were either one or the other! So, because you are lukewarm—neither hot nor cold—I am about to spit you out of my mouth" (Revelation 3:15–16). That was the harshest criticism of all the churches because they chose comfort over following Jesus.

I can understand wanting comfort over putting yourself out there and being vulnerable to attack. One may think they are "on fire for Christ," meaning they are actively pursuing God and his will. However, when the temperature is turned up, when we are tested in that faithfulness, it shows our true beliefs. I can testify to that experience firsthand. Several years ago, I was not just attending church, but also involved with what felt like every possible group. I was on the worship team, helped with fellowship events, on the church board, helped with property projects, served as both a deacon and elder, and led a women's group. While those were ways I was able to serve for the time I did, God had a bigger plan for me in my dream of writing. That required me to scale back my duties in church almost completely. My roles at church had become a part of my identity, and I was in my comfort zone in how I served God. I was stuck trying to stoke a fire that God wanted me to douse and move on. The lesson is to trust in where God is leading us to serve, even if it means closing a door to past activities to allow for a new one to open.

When I began my writing journey, the attacks from the enemy stepped up. Because I wasn't fully aware of what those would look like, I wasn't equipped to defend against them. I remember my first conversation with my book designer, Tami, when she warned me about the attacks and said she would be praying for me. I responded, "I have already been dealing with that," but this was just the beginning of my awareness of the attacks. As I have continued my writing journey, now sharing my story on podcasts and sermon messages, the heat has turned up more. My calling as a writer has pushed me farther outside of my comfort zone. In those challenges, all we can do is trust that God is with us to guide us. We can fight the enemy's fire with the fire of Christ in us.

While I am still learning how to deflect the enemy's attempts to discourage me, I have found many moments where God had prepared me for this. While going through some cards I had received over the years, I found this treasure that said, in part, "Ministry is a funny thing. It can burn one out or really revive the soul, to find the balance is hard and takes time. Often times there can be a lot of 'failures' involved before 'success.' We [may] often wonder 'am I making a difference?' Rest assured you are, even if you only transform yourself, it is worth it. You are a very unique and powerful young woman. I see great and wonderful things stirring deep within you."[41] While my burnout from worship team still brings sadness, I can also see where writing revives my soul.

While you may not be called to slay an actual Goliath, we all fight some kind of battle. Whether it's a physical ailment, mental health struggles, challenging jobs, or relationships, we need to use our tools from God, including prayer. The enemy will try to derail us from sharing the good news in whatever form that is, such as serving the homeless, taking a meal to a sick friend, or listening to a friend vent about a problem. Using our shield of faith to both defend and attack is how we can win those little battles. Thankfully, in the end, God wins the final battle.

REFLECTION QUESTIONS:

1. *How have you used the tool of prayer to defend against the enemy?*

2. *What area of serving God has you on fire for Christ?*

Read John 17 and thank Jesus for his prayers.

Song: "Overthinking"

by Samantha Ebert

(39.) John Berridge, "John Berridge to Samuel Wilks, Everton, August 16, 1774," *The Works of the Rev. John Berridge, A.M.*, ed. Richard Whittingham, Simpkin, Marshall, and Co., 1838, p 396.

(40.) Priscilla Shirer, *The Armor of God*, Nashville, TN: LifeWay Press, 2015, p. 125.

(41.) Personal card from Paul Tilton, November 1, 1997.

18

SAILING INTO THE SUNSET

"Faith doesn't always take you out of the problem, it takes you through the problem. Faith doesn't always take away the pain, it gives you the ability to handle the pain. Faith doesn't always take you out of the storm, it calms you in the midst of the storm." [42]

OUR NEXT STEP IS putting all our ships into action and living out our faith. We have the examples of Jesus and Stephen to show us how to remain faithful, and Peter to show us we can be renewed in faithfulness by turning back to God in repentance. It takes effort every day of our lives until God calls us home.

Our best example of remaining faithful is Jesus in his final hours. While he prayed for God to take the cup from him, he also said, "Yet not as I will, but as you will" (Matthew

26:39). Jesus had many opportunities to bow out, to call on angels to save him, but he knew doing that would not result in our salvation. Aren't we glad Jesus obeyed God and saved us from our sins? He went through all the trials, mocking, lashes, carrying his own cross, crucifixion, and death to bridge the gap created by sin between mankind and God.

"Sometimes the hardest thing you will do as a human is say 'thy will be done' and give something to God. We naturally want to handle the problem on our own, solve it immediately, and have all the answers. As a follower of Christ, that is not how it works. You have to give up the thought that you have the power and remember that you are supposed to be relying on the power of Christ, the one who redeems, restores, fulfills, and heals. It is not our will, but his. Let go, and see what GOD is wanting to do."[43]

While hanging on the cross, Jesus had limited breath so could only say a few words at a time. One of those things he said was, "My God, My God, why have you forsaken me?" (Psalm 22:1). Those are powerful words to choose as Jesus took on the weight of our sins. We can feel the desperation, anguish, and even abandonment in those lines. When I was suicidal, it felt like even God had left me. Those were the darkest moments of my life.

However, Jesus encourages us to read the entire psalm, which shows a more complete picture of his story. The psalm shows us that we can take all our emotions and thoughts to

God, no matter how heavy. While the psalm starts out as a cry, it ends in a proclamation. "They will proclaim his righteousness, declaring to a people yet unborn: He has done it!" (Psalm 22:31). While everyone thought the story of Jesus was done when he breathed his last breath, it was just the beginning.

Stephen showed his faithfulness to the end, becoming the first Christian martyr. He was described as "a man full of God's grace and power" (Acts 6:8). Stephen was brought before the Sanhedrin (the Jewish leaders). He was guided by the Holy Spirit to show them, through the Scriptures, how they killed the Messiah they had been waiting for. "His hearers [the Sanhedrin] reacted with great rage, realizing that he had used their own Scriptures to accuse them."[44] Not surprisingly, they decided to stone him to death. Stephen was faithful until his last breath, even showing forgiveness to his killers by saying, "Lord, do not hold this sin against them" (Acts 7:60). What a final prayer to God, asking for forgiveness for his persecutors!

While Stephen powerfully showed his faith at his death, Peter knew he had failed at the moment when Jesus needed him most. Peter denied he knew Jesus after Jesus was taken into custody, just as Jesus predicted. The disciples went from knowing that Jesus was crucified to seeing he was risen from the dead. Being in Jesus's presence again must have been wonderful, yet I can imagine Peter carried the guilt of those denials. At the end of the Gospel of John, Jesus asked Peter three times, "Do you love me?" Peter was enthusiastic at first, but by the third time, appeared frustrated by the same question. But this was meant for Peter to confirm his love and commitment to Jesus the exact number of times he denied his Savior, renewing his faith. The life of a believer can push us to follow Jesus to places we would rather not go, but we can show our faithfulness by going anyway.

A few months before my father-in-law passed away, a group of us took him ziplining. He was ninety-four years old, but was willing to give it a go. Ziplining requires a lot of trust. Once you get hooked onto the line, you then have to step off the block, which is a step of faith. Thankfully, we had some instruction and preparation in how to slow down, if needed. But the more important piece was how to pull yourself to the end of the line so you didn't get stuck on the course. Generally speaking, if you can feel confident in what you have learned, you can enjoy the ride. While I enjoyed the day, it was almost more fun to watch my father-in-law having a blast. Unfortunately, there was a lot of walking on a hot summer day, so he didn't finish with us. That adventure was one of his last big challenges and inspires me to keep pushing myself out of my comfort zone and try new things. Since God is with us every step, we can enjoy the ride of life.

Being a Christian starts with saying yes and getting on board with Christ. There is no retirement age. We can use these examples as a reminder to keep showing faithfulness until our final sail into the sunset when God calls us home.

REFLECTION QUESTIONS:

1. *Read Psalm 22. How does that change your view of what Jesus said on the cross?*

2. *How has this book helped you deepen your faith?*

Go and serve God every day.

Song: "Oh Death"

by MercyMe

(42.) Clergy Coaching Network the FORUM, "Faith doesn't always take out of the problem," Facebook, January 28, 2025, https://www.facebook.com/clergycoachingnetwork/posts/pfbid02g7vtgdzWcYecxhfEFBCSzc3w WFbjBgkeDt2GK9orDoEDNm15EigtF5iY6JmNJ9gEl.

(43.) Servant Hearted Sisterhood, "Sometimes the hardest thing," Facebook, May 10, 2025, 2025, https://www.facebook.com/servantheartedsisterhood/posts/pfbid02qvayWhFto7Bd9uYKENTKRdXwp949a7JCMqYXRx K4soSLgoGGAWsCBHwK8QRqBrjPl.

(44.) *NIV Quest Study Bible*, Grand Rapids, MI: Zondervan, 2001, p. 1621.